BUILDING
BY THE BOOK

PATTERN BOOK ARCHITECTURE IN NEW JERSEY

BUILDING
BY THE
BOOK

Robert P. Guter

Janet W. Foster

PHOTOGRAPHS BY

Jim DelGiudice

Rutgers University Press
New Brunswick, New Jersey

Publication of this book was made possible, in part, by a grant from the New Jersey
Committee for the Humanities, a state program of the National Endowment for the
Humanities.

The opinions, findings, and conclusions or recommendations expressed in this book are
those of the authors, and do not necessarily reflect those of the NJCH or the NEH.

The original work upon which this book is based was done on behalf of the Middlesex
County Cultural and Heritage Commission, for their exhibit "Building by the Book: New
Jersey Pattern-Book Architecture," October 1988–April 1989.

Unless specifically stated otherwise, the houses depicted in this book are private
residences and are not open to the public. The authors ask that readers respect the privacy
of those whose homes have been included here.

Library of Congress Cataloging-in-Publication Data

Guter, Robert P.
    Building by the book : pattern-book architecture in New Jersey /
Robert P. Guter, Janet W. Foster ; photographs by Jim DelGiudice.
       p. cm.
    Includes bibliographical references and index.
    ISBN 0-8135-1848-2
    1. Architecture, Domestic—New Jersey—Designs and plans.
  I. Foster, Janet W. II. DelGiudice, Jim. III. Title.
NA7235.N5G87 1992
728'.37'09749—dc20   92-6516
                                      CIP

*For
G.O. and J.F.,
whose patience never wore thin*

Contents

Preface

At the age of twelve, I rescued from a trash can a large book filled with pictures of old houses. Years later, I realized that a house that looked exactly like the first plate in the book stood only a block from my home, and I discovered that the book itself was the now rare *How to Build, Furnish, and Decorate,* by Robert Shoppell, one of the late nineteenth-century's mass merchandisers of house plans.

From my work as a planner and preservationist and my studies of New Jersey architecture and the built environment, it became clear to me that certain houses were nearly identical to one another, although they stood miles apart. It was only in graduate school that I began to understand why. The world of architectural pattern books was revealed to me in the depths of Avery Library at Columbia University—and I began to find the published sources for familiar buildings.

In 1984 Janet Foster joined me in forming Acroterion, a firm devoted to the research, documentation, and preservation of historic buildings. One of our first large projects was a survey of historic resources throughout Morris County. Describing and photographing every building in the county more than fifty years old was not only a herculean task of organization and stamina, but it brought again to the fore the remarkable similarities of some houses to each other, and in some cases, to printed sources.

At about the time we were laboring over the Morris County Survey, the Preservation Press of the National Trust for Historic Preservation published *Houses by Mail,* an account of the more than four hundred house models sold by Sears, Roebuck and Company in the first third of the twentieth century. So many were identifiable in the neighborhoods we were surveying that we came to recognize particular models, such as the Crescent, instantly.

When the Middlesex County Cultural and Heritage Commission asked us in the winter of 1988 if we would like to serve as guest curators of an exhibit on New Jersey architecture, we knew immediately what our topic would be—pattern books and their influence on the buildings that have survived to make up New Jersey's landscape today. The bits of information we had collected almost randomly over the years were now called forth, and we eagerly seized the opportunity to pursue the pattern-book subject in depth. The result, an exhibit at the Middlesex County Museum in the Cornelius Low House, was titled *Building by the Book* and ran for six months. Through photographs, reproductions of pattern-book plates, architectural models, and artifacts of the buildings themselves, we made a strong case for the direct influence of pattern books on New Jersey architecture.

The exhibit closed in April 1989, but our curiosity was merely piqued, not satisfied. We asked Rutgers University Press if they might consider publishing a summary or catalog of the exhibit, so that the information we had collected could be preserved in some way. Leslie Mitchner, who became our editor, went considerably further by offering us the opportunity to write this book. Some information survived the transition from exhibit to book, but much of it is new, and, we believe, even more forceful in making the point of the importance of published sources on New Jersey's architectural landscape.

Robert P. Guter
Janet W. Foster
MORRISTOWN, 1992

Building the Book: A Photographer's Perspective

On a hot summer day I discover something magical on the back roads of New Jersey. Beneath a humid sky I realize that this is my home. Considering that it has taken an odyssey of three years and four thousand miles for this revelation to occur, I should not now be amazed. The discovery shocks me nonetheless, because it isn't what I was looking for at all.

My association with Robert Guter began a decade ago, when, on a whim, I attended a lecture he gave on pattern-book architecture. I was just beginning to photograph seriously, and the insights I gained into the value of historic preservation focused my thoughts about photographing buildings in their environments. A series of collaborations followed, most notably documentation for the nomination of Llewellyn Park in West Orange to the National Register of Historic Places. But during my initial, fruitless visits to that designed Romantic community, I began to see how little I knew about photographing a planned architectural landscape. How could my twentieth-century eye portray, through a twentieth-century lens, the Victorian aphorism of "a place for everything and everything in its place"? As a result of (or perhaps in spite of) my efforts, Bob and his business partner, Janet Foster, continued to come back for more. In 1988 they asked me to provide photography for a significant museum exhibit, not surprisingly on the subject of pattern-book architecture. The outgrowth of that exhibit—and the result of three years' travel through New Jersey's past—is my work in *Building by the Book*.

Eminent New Jersey photographer George Tice, in his introduction to *Urban Landscapes* (Rutgers University Press, 1975), wrote that his challenge "was how to take interesting, expressive photographs of the most ordinary subjects that I, for some reason, felt worthy of documentation." The subjects in *Building by the Book* are not "found" objects: if they were vernacular in their time, they are most certainly not ordinary today, although they may sometimes seem so as we rush blindly past them. Some of the buildings are, in fact, unique enough to have been documented and protected as historic landmarks. My photographic problem, then, became the opposite of Tice's: to express something valuable about identifiable, assigned subjects, in a sense to *idealize* them by matching them to patterns.

Unfortunately, these residences no longer sit serenely in romantic landscapes like Llewellyn Park. Enclosed today by ever-shrinking environmental bubbles, they maintain an uneasy truce with the surrounding visual chaos of the late twentieth century. Antennas, air conditioners, street signs, cables, overgrown shrubs, and abutting new structures, along with the deferred maintenance typical of the current economic climate, all intruded on the idealization I sought. I constantly exhort students to strive for "impact" in their photographs. But such advice came to haunt me during my expeditions across New Jersey. The potential for bizarre photographic compositions was everywhere, but, unlike Tice, I couldn't embrace it. A row of decapitated trees forming a ruined colonnade around a Greek Revival mansion was poignant; Halloween decorations on a pagoda-style cottage were comical. Other juxtapositions were more disturbing. As a colleague accurately put it, "There's something unnerving about standing on the shaded property of the stately Hermitage in Ho-Ho-Kus and being assaulted by the smell of a nearby fast-food restaurant and the noise of highway traffic."

While great buildings like the Hermitage endure, albeit as monuments rather than private homes, I am concerned for the future of the less-known and less-protected dwellings found in these pages. My fear for their survival, which had its genesis so long ago, has not abated, but has grown with the revelations I've experienced in my journey. I hope that this book is a reminder of how much our past defines us. If these buildings disappear, yet another link with that past will be broken; and the quality of life in this state which we call home will be immeasurably reduced.

Jim DelGiudice
CONVENT STATION, 1992

Acknowledgments

Although we did not know it then, this book began its existence in 1988 when Anna Aschkenes, executive director of the Middlesex County Cultural and Heritage Commission, invited us to serve as guest curators for an exhibit devoted to New Jersey architecture at the Middlesex County Museum. We are grateful to her for believing that we had seven rooms' worth of things to say. The support of the commission and the help of Susan Kittredge, assistant director, and Kyle Nardelli, historic sites supervisor of the Cornelius Low House, encouraged us to enlarge the scope of the exhibit and find a way to preserve its findings.

A good exhibit does not necessarily make a good book. The generous support of the New Jersey Historical Commission enabled us to travel throughout New Jersey to find additional pattern-book houses and to carry out the research necessary to document them.

Without the tenacity, prodigious research skills, and good humor of Suzanne Benton, our resolve to forge ahead would more than once have evaporated. Sandy and Don Hamingson helped us bring order from a chaotic pile of manuscript, and guided us through many tense moments—both past and historical present. Constance M. Greiff read the completed manuscript with unusual care, helping us to draw distinctions we otherwise would have overlooked.

Without help from the keepers of several important collections, we would have been unable to make essential visual and historical connections. We especially thank: William Dane of the

Fine Arts Collection of the Newark Public Library, for sharing with enthusiasm the library's collection of original pattern books; Angela Giral and her staff at the Avery Architectural and Fine Arts Library, Columbia University in the City of New York, for making the collection accessible and facilitating photo reproduction; Roger Moss, director, the Athenaeum of Philadelphia, who helped with important sources on last-minute notice; Diana Cheng and her staff at the Local History Room of the Joint Free Public Library of Morristown and Morris Township, for careful custody of a rich collection and help with illustrations; the Office of Special Collections at the New York Public Library, for a very special collection and permission to reproduce illustrations.

Several of New Jersey's most important historic house museums are among the pattern-book houses analyzed in the following pages. We thank them and their administrators for help with research and permission to photograph: Acorn Hall, Jeanne Watson; Thomas Edison National Historic Site, George Tselos; the Hermitage, Florence Leon; Historic Speedwell, Sarah Henrich; Pomona Hall, Margaret Wetherill; Proprietary House, Alma Cap; the Willows at Fosterfields, Nancy Strathearn and the Morris County Park Commission.

Friends, colleagues, and historic-house owners were generous with information about buildings, pattern books, historic photographs, and research sources: Virginia Borsner, Millburn; T. Robbins Brown, Bergen County Office of Cultural and Historic Affairs; Lauren Brunski, Shrewsbury; Richard and Elizabeth Diefenthaler, Chatham; Randall Gabrielan, Middletown; John Grady, Plainfield; Mr. and Mrs. Robert Hill, Metuchen; Carl Holm, Bridgeton; Terry Karschner, Trenton; Bates and Isabel Lowry, Stuart, Florida; Melinda McGough, Haddonfield; Virginia Mosley, Tenafly; Bierce Reilly, Morristown; William Redmond, Friendship, Maine; Emil Salvini, Pompton Plains; John Steen, Mountain Lakes; Ray Stubblebine, Oradell; Linda Smith, Mount Tabor; Ann and James Yardley, Morristown.

Sears, Roebuck and Company granted permission to reproduce illustrations from Sears House Catalogs; Patricia S. Eldredge, archivist for the Sherwin-Williams Company, helped secure permission to reproduce the illustration that serves as the glossary.

Many of the illustrations in this book are from reprints of pattern books. The original title of the pattern book in question is noted in the caption; a fuller citation, including the name of the modern publisher, is available in the bibliography. When an original pattern book was photocopied to supply an illustration, the library or individual who owns the book is credited. All photographs are by Jim DelGiudice except where noted. These exceptions are historic photos, and their owners are credited because in most cases the original photographer is unknown. Jim would like to acknowl-

edge the invaluable assistance of his friend and colleague, the late
George Scinto.

Rutgers University Press made the work of writing and producing this book a pleasure. Leslie Mitchner, our editor, was a
constant source of encouragement. Marilyn Campbell and Willa
Speiser helped us to say what we meant. The difficult challenge of
turning a very visual subject into a book that communicates through
its images was met ably by John Romer and Barbara Kopel.

BUILDING
BY THE BOOK

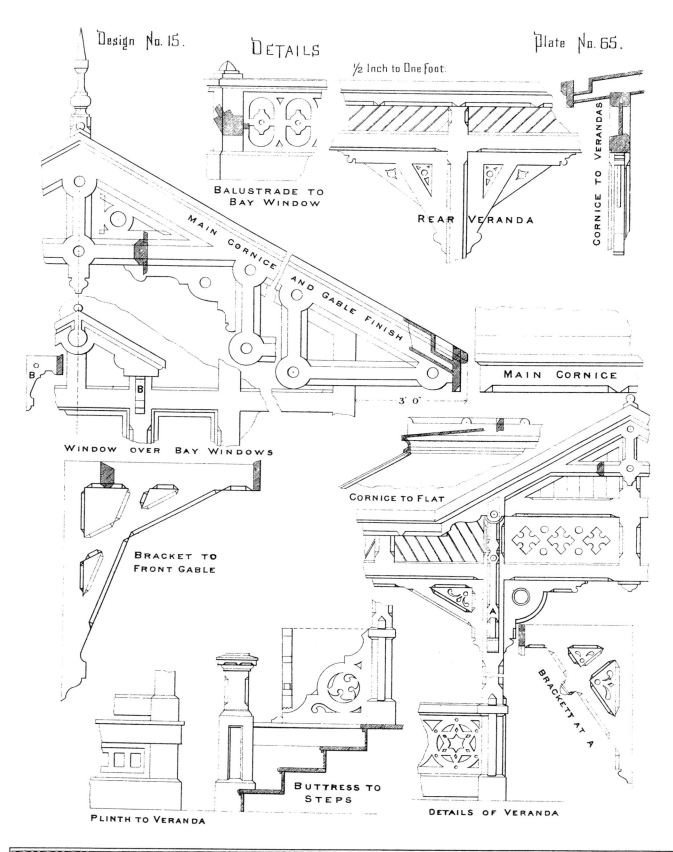

Design No. 15.   Details   Plate No. 65.

½ Inch to One Foot.

BALUSTRADE TO
BAY WINDOW

REAR VERANDA

CORNICE TO VERANDAS

MAIN CORNICE AND GABLE FINISH

B

B

3' 0"

MAIN CORNICE

WINDOW OVER BAY WINDOWS

CORNICE TO FLAT

BRACKET TO
FRONT GABLE

BRACKETT AT A

PLINTH TO VERANDA

BUTTRESS TO
STEPS

DETAILS OF VERANDA

INTRODUCTION

One of the first wants of a person desirous of building an ornamental Cottage or Villa is a Book of Designs, which shall
convey to his eye representations of what is either beautiful or convenient. From such previously formed ideas, he
embodies his own conceptions of the ornamental and useful, and learns what will be the most suitable.
   Thomas Ustick Walter, *Two Hundred Designs for Cottages
   & Villas*, 1847

Thomas U. Walter's forthright advice reminds us that before the rise
of the architectural profession, building by the book was commonplace. Almost every New Jersey town that reached maturity sometime between the Civil War and World War II owes much of its
appearance to published sources, both written and pictorial. Books
(and later, magazines) instructed generations of builders and their
clients in matters of taste and technology. Enlightened by such
cheap and readily available sources, middle-class homeowners chose
everything from the latest architectural style to the paint colors that

would flatter it. How to build, furnish, and decorate (the title of an 1880s book), became a topic of fervid interest throughout the nineteenth century. But the influence of published sources on New Jersey buildings began in the eighteenth century, when every gentleman was expected to know something about the art of architecture.

The earliest architectural books available in colonial New Jersey were influential beyond their small number. Read by a group of wealthy and well-educated men, these sumptuous folios, published in England, were often graced with Latin titles, such as *Vitruvius Britannicus*. They gave the gentleman amateur instruction in the classical orders and offered engravings of noble estates to suggest how the ancient orders might be employed to produce modern country seats. Although we customarily associate these grand Palladian mansions of the Georgian period with Tidewater Virginia, they were built in New Jersey, too. But to build a great country seat, a richly illustrated folio was not sufficient. At the opposite end of the book-publishing scale was another kind of book entirely, a small volume, sized to fit in a carpenter's pocket. Filled with practical instructions and detailed illustrations, these little books showed a workman how to accomplish the grand ambitions his patron had imagined—how, in effect, to get things built. In his important bibliography, *American Architectural Books*, Henry-Russell Hitchcock calls these small books "builders' guides," which he defines as books "where the graphic material consists chiefly of plates of the [classical architectural] orders, together with other plates showing elements of detail both structural and ornamental."

The importance of printed sources was evident even in prestigious commissions. William Thornton, a medical doctor who, in 1793, won the competition for designing the United States Capitol, remarked, "I got some books and worked for a few days, then gave a plan in the ancient Ionic order, which carried the day." *The Country Builder's Assistant*, by Asher Benjamin, was published in 1797; it was the first builders' guide by an American author. Benjamin and his younger colleague, Minard Lafever (born near Morristown, New Jersey, in 1798), began with simple handbooks that focused on practical construction problems. Their first books presented Federal-style designs, but by the 1830s both had become energetic popularizers of the Greek Revival style. Transitional in format, these early books of Benjamin and Lafever were larger than the English builders' books that had preceded them; they included a few plans and elevations and attempted an American perspective, but remained decidedly dry and old-fashioned. Most important, they were written for country carpenters, not the carpenters' clients. These books, despite their conservative outlook, contained essential and handsome illustrations that helped to change the way New Jersey houses were built during the first four decades of the nineteeth century, as even a casual look at Flemington, Princeton, Morristown, or a score of other towns will prove.

By the middle of the 1840s a new kind of book ushered in the era of "house pattern books" as Hitchcock dubbed them, or simply "pattern books" as we have come to call them. For the first time, architectural books were being written expressly for house consumers rather than builders. Instead of advice on structural problems and geometrical computations, the new books found a mass market by publishing plans and elevations to stimulate the architectural appetite of a burgeoning middle class in search of comfort and good taste. One man stood at the center of this important change: Andrew Jackson Downing. Downing's first full-fledged architectural book, *Cottage Residences*, appeared in 1842 and was taken up immediately by New Jersey home owners who were in the vanguard of a new and uniquely American way of living—suburbia. Instead of instructions for carpenters, Downing emphasized engravings of picturesque dwellings in equally picturesque landscapes, with floor plans, details of porches, chimneys, and bargeboards, and a text that offered practical and philosophical justifications for a new kind of architecture, one devised for the American scene. With their effective integration of text and pictures, Downing and his peers accomplished two things: they promoted the integration of the domestic arts—architecture, interior decoration, and landscape design, and they broke decisively from the stranglehold of classicism to reinvigorate American architecture with a Romantic outlook.

The period from about 1840 until the Civil War was the first Golden Age of the American architectural pattern book. In New Jersey the Italianate and Gothic Revival styles became enormously popular as readers built avidly from designs in such influential books as A. J. Downing's *The Architecture of Country Houses* (1850), Samuel Sloan's *The Model Architect* (1852), Gervase Wheeler's *Homes for the People in Suburb and Country* (1855), Calvert Vaux's *Villas and Cottages* (1857), and George E. Woodward's *Woodward's Country Homes* (1865). As post–Civil War affluence whetted the public's architectural appetite, publishers competed to satisfy it with the help of new inventions, bringing pattern-book-built houses to an ever larger New Jersey audience. Pattern books filled with more numerous engravings rolled off steam-powered presses for distribution to the smallest towns via steam-powered trains. The old regional differences in architecture began to fade when readers as far distant as Cape May and Hackettstown were inspired by the same pattern-book designs.

Unlike the gentleman amateur of the eighteenth century who designed his own dwelling with the help of separate elements culled from an expensive folio, the average pattern-book buyer of the second half of the nineteenth century, whether carpenter or client, was looking for a model more or less "off the shelf." This kind of market insured that many published designs were cranked out expressly for a mass audience, although some books included houses already built for specific clients, designs intended for general inspiration or direct emulation. Some home builders attempted line-for-line copies of published designs, but in other cases owners and their carpenters made adjustments based on personal taste, differing practical requirements, and the availability of materials—a practice encouraged by most pattern-book authors.

As early as the 1840s, building by the book had been promoted by magazines as well as pattern books proper. Important in this effort was *Godey's Magazine*, later known as *Godey's Lady's Book*, probably the most widely circulated monthly magazine in America between 1840 and 1860. In addition to needlework patterns, recipes, sentimental stories, and colored engravings of the latest fashions, *Godey's* published house plans and elevations reprinted from the most popular pattern books or commissioned especially for the magazine. Another periodical, the *American Agriculturist*, brought up-to-date house plans to farmers. New Jersey readers of this important agricultural journal built farmhouses from its pages in places like Rocky Hill, Freehold, and Allentown.

By the last quarter of the nineteenth century, "railroad suburbs" were plentiful in New Jersey. The statewide building boom that helped to create them in Dunellen, Madison, Plainfield, Tenafly, and dozens more suburban towns was based on the firm foundation of the earliest pattern books, but architectural styles had taken off into flights of fanciful eclecticism since the era of Downing. *Modern Dwellings in Town and Country*, for example, an 1878 pattern book by Henry Hudson Holly, brought before the building public the latest architectural truth, that of the English Aesthetic movement, translated into American terms. Although English critics and tastemakers like John Ruskin, William Morris, and Charles Eastlake might disavow the transatlantic results of their theories, American homeowners were quick to embrace the Stick Style, the Queen Anne style, and the Shingle Style. In doing so, they moved away from the relative simplicity of the Italianate and Gothic modes, creating New Jersey streetscapes and entire neighborhoods filled with rambunctious dwellings that burst out of the traditional architectural box. Their bays, angles, ells, porches, towers and turrets, hipped roofs, pyramidal roofs, mansards, shingle, clapboard, brick, terra cotta, slate, stained glass, and cast iron proclaimed the emancipation of architecture from preconceived notions of "appropriateness" and, some claimed, from the canons of "good taste."

This era of pattern-book eclecticism created the houses we think of most readily as "Victorian." Once more, cause and effect are difficult to separate, but it cannot be denied that this was also the greatest era of architectural mass marketing that the nation had seen. In the year 1871 American publishers brought out eight architectural books, while in 1882 the number had jumped to twenty. Available from the local bookseller or through the mail, a host of large-format, relatively inexpensive pattern books overflowed with hundreds of house designs and details. Some of the architectural authors most associated with this Era of Extravagance are D. T. Atwood, Amos Jackson Bicknell, William Thompkins Comstock, E. C. Hussey, Palliser and Palliser, George E. Woodward, and Robert W. Shoppell, most of whom wrote or published multiple titles. In addition to their published designs, the Pallisers and others began to offer complete house plans and specifications by mail for a modest charge.

Because of its position between the great metropolitan centers of New York and Philadelphia, New Jersey was the suburban conduit that carried much of this pattern-book intelligence and saw it produce built examples. In the 1870s and 1880s a veritable colony of pattern-book authors lived in Bergen County, where several towns became laboratories for their work. Both George Woodward (author of *Country Homes*, 1865) and Elisha Hussey (who wrote *Home Building* in 1876) maintained New York City offices but settled their families in Rutherford, a burgeoning railroad suburb, where houses from their designs were built. At about the same time, Daniel T. Atwood expanded his New York City architectural practice to New Jersey, where he became a developer as well when he bought a large farm tract for subdivision in Tenafly. Many of the houses he built there appeared in *Atwood's Country and Suburban Houses* (1871) and *Atwood's Modern American Homesteads* (1876). S. Burrage Reed, author of *House Plans for Everybody* (1890), was the first mayor of Woodcliff Lake. *Suburban Architecture*, written in 1894 by William Lambert, who had offices in Hackensack and Nutley as well as New York City, illustrated a number of his Bergen County buildings.

The proliferation of pattern books and the density of New Jersey development by the turn of the century complicates the task of matching built examples to pattern-book designs. The purpose of pattern books was changing, too. With the increase of trained architects as well as architect-author-promoters like Atwood and the Pallisers, who sold house plans outright, the need to educate provincial carpenters and potential house buyers through the pages of pattern books grew less urgent.

Despite this shift of emphasis, the potency of architectural visualization in books and popular periodicals continued into the twentieth century. Gustav Stickley, who made his home in Morris Plains from 1908 until 1917, featured house plans in *The Craftsman*, his influential monthly magazine, beginning in 1903. New Jersey suburbanites adopted Stickley's Arts and Crafts plainness with enthusiasm, building by the dozens modest but well-planned cottages and bungalows from the pages of *The Craftsman*. Concurrent with Stickley's popularity, but outlasting it, was the architectural arm of Sears, Roebuck and Company, which improved on Palliser and Palliser's marketing techniques by offering entire ready-cut houses (not merely plans), delivered to your local railroad station in pieces, ready for assembly. Building by the book reached its logical conclusion in New Jersey as thousands of consumers pored over the illustrated catalogs of Sears and other manufacturers to order houses by mail.

Mail-order plans and ready-cut houses fulfilled their promoters' dreams of furnishing sound housing at reasonable cost to thousands of Americans. To some, the potential of factory-built housing had seemed limitless, but the Great Depression brought building of all kinds to a virtual standstill. During the 1930s lumberyards, contractors, and even the building department of Sears, Roebuck went out of business. In 1934, in an effort to revive the construction industry and stimulate home purchases, the United States government created the Federal Housing Administration (FHA). The long-term, low-interest loans that Americans learned to take for granted were an FHA innovation. The first FHA-insured mortgage was approved for a house in Pequannock, New Jersey, in 1934.

Although the buildup of defense industries during World War II returned the American economy to health, home building was deferred for lack of manpower and materials. With peace, the pent-up housing demand of nearly fifteen years transformed the New Jersey landscape. Because the overwhelming need for new housing had to be met faster than individual families could manage, mass production was the only solution. Farms became housing developments, and drive-in strips grew up to serve them, threatening the health of traditional Main Streets everywhere they spread.

Behind this mass production was a new breed of builder-developer, often operating on an immense scale and always looking for ways to cut costs. The most effective economy was to offer one or two basic house types, with distinguishing features expressed only in applied details. By repeating the same house over and over, the developer could minimize design fees and save additional money by using standard fittings.

Large developers might hire their own architects; smaller developers could turn to catalogs published by construction companies, mail-order design services, and local building-trade associations. These were aimed exclusively at the builder, whose choice of designs was influenced by his presumably conservative buyers and the unquestionably conservative outlook of the FHA, which was loath to insure a mortgage on any house that looked unfamiliar. As a result, the builders' catalogs became repositories of safe, traditional design, unlike the best of the nineteenth-century pattern books, which took their readers into unexplored architectural territory.

Now, at the end of the twentieth century, domestic architecture in New Jersey and the rest of the country has reverted to something very like the dual system of the eighteenth century. Wealthy clients are the patrons of new architecture, while most of us live in vernacular buildings. Our new vernacular houses, of course, are created not out of a folk tradition but from designs made expressly to further the economic aims of developers. In this rough-and-tumble world of the bottom line and what usually seems like the least common denominator aesthetically, the influence of the nineteenth-century pattern book persists nonetheless. One of its legacies is the expectation, never more difficult to fulfill, that every American should be able to own a single-family house on its own green acre. Another is the belief that housing can influence the actions of its inhabitants, more pointedly that good houses make good citizens. From the pattern books of Andrew Jackson Downing to the Craftsman homes of Gustav Stickley, that assumption has been an underlying theme of building by the book. That moral imperative is part of New Jersey's suburban history and its unfulfilled promise.

1

FROM BUILDERS' BOOKS TO PATTERN BOOKS

Eighteenth-Century Beginnings

On Friday, January 8, 1802, Stephen Youngs of Hanover, Morris County, New Jersey, wrote in his memorandum book: "Thatched the Roof of my cowhouse, stuck a thorn in my finger which hurt very much. I finished at about dusk."[1]

The unfortunate Stephen recovered from his stuck finger to live a long and busy life; he died in 1867 at the age of ninety-three. Like most of his neighbors, he was a farmer; but he was a carpenter as well. He learned the trade of carpenter-builder both from his father and through a formal apprenticeship. Stephen was heir to traditional building practices, including thatching, which had been transmitted from father to son, from England to America, for generations. The houses he built were sturdy but uncomplicated, influenced more by need than by ideas of symmetry or style.

Such was the state of architecture throughout New Jersey at the turn of the eighteenth century, when ordinary houses were products of craftsmanship untouched by the architect's hand (Fig. 1). Wood was the most popular building material by far, although German, Dutch, and Quaker settlers contributed important stone and brick exceptions to the wooden rule. Most builders could afford to concern themselves with little more than shelter—keeping out the rain and keeping in the heat. In response to these basic necessities they fashioned dwellings out of their own distinctive European folk-building traditions, modified by the conditions and materials at hand. It was this practical view of life that prompted the high-born Mrs. Martha Daingerfield Bland, on the eve of the Revolution, to call the inhabitants of one New Jersey country town "the errantest rustics you ever beheld." [2] Even if such "rustics" had been concerned with the niceties of ornament and classical symmetry, they would have found no architects to translate their impulses into architecture.

At around the time of the Revolution, residents of the state's few urbanized places (they could barely be called cities) were building houses not quite as rude as those of their country cousins. In places like Burlington, Elizabeth, and Perth Amboy, late-eighteenth-century prosperity enabled successful merchants and skilled craftsmen to live in neat dwellings set among gardens and orchards, but the high art of architecture was available only to the very wealthy. Thomas Thompson, an Anglican missionary writing in 1756, was a guest at some few houses of the "Jersey gentry." These, he remarked, had a "large thorow entry" where the wife and daughters sat at work "like Minerva and her nymphs, without headdress, gown, shoes or stockings." [3] Stuffed full of classical allusions by his Cambridge education, Thompson was describing the capacious center hall of a Georgian mansion house like the one completed in 1776 for Jacob Ford, Jr., and his family in Morristown

Fig. 1. In 1844 when Deckertown was pictured in Historical Collections of the State of New Jersey, *it was typical of many New Jersey villages that had changed little since the eighteenth century. Only the churches, the hotel, and one large dwelling betrayed a hint of high-style architecture; the rest of the houses were devoid of conscious "taste."*

Fig. 2. Jacob Ford, Jr., saw to it that his simplified Palladian villa was embellished with fine wooden ornament. Because of its associations with George Washington, Robert Sears included the Ford house in his Pictorial Description of the United States, *published in 1848.*

(Fig. 2). Here was high-style architecture a world removed from the folk-building traditions of the yeoman population. How Jacob Ford's house came to be built tells us a good deal about the influence of printed sources on New Jersey architecture of the eighteenth century.

New Jersey architecture for the ruling class was English architecture transplanted, and that English architecture would have been impossible without architectural books. The wellspring of both the buildings and the books that promoted them was one man, the Italian architect Andrea Palladio (1508–1580). In his 1570 treatise, *Quattro Libri dell' Architettura*, rendered into English in 1714 as *The Four Books of Architecture*, Palladio demonstrated his skill at using a classical architectural language that could be adapted for different needs, his grasp of ingenious and practical planning ideas, and his genius for forceful composition. American Palladianism was modified by exposure to English books such as Colen

Campbell's *Vitruvius Britannicus* (1715) and James Gibbs's *A Book of Architecture* (1728), both filled with new designs based on Palladian precedents. Numbered among the American buyers of such books were the best-educated and most powerful men in the colonies. The books they bought were not popular in the sense of enjoying a wide distribution, but they were enormously influential among the cognoscenti who read them. Thomas Jefferson, although the most famous and talented of the gentlemen-architects who sought inspiration from these books, was by no means atypical. Writing to a friend in 1804, he boasted, "There never was a Palladio here even in private hands till I bought one."[4]

Palladian books fell into two categories. First were the sumptuous folios like *Vitruvius Britannicus* for the gentleman amateur like Jacob Ford, who might collaborate on the design of his own dwelling. Practical dissemination of the Palladian wisdom they contained, however, was the job of dozens of inexpensive handbooks, small enough to fit in the pocket of a carpenter's breeches. One of the most prolific handbook authors was an Englishman named Batty Langley, who explained in his 1741 book, *The Builder's Jewel*, "As those books [the folios] are of large price and beyond the reach of many . . . I have here extracted . . . all that is useful for workmen." Batty Langley and others wrote books that were long on structure and geometry. They might even include illustrations of the five orders of architecture, so essential to the entire classical system, but they made no attempt to compete with the folios by offering elaborate plans and elevations.

In light of their availability to men of means, it is reasonable to assume that Jacob Ford might have owned a Palladian folio and his housewright a Palladian handbook, but without his library inventory in hand, how certain can we be of Ford's debt to printed Palladian sources? Even a casual examination of his mansion house lays all doubts to rest. Its basic composition, with main block and subsidiary service wing, is a greatly simplified but instantly recognizable Palladian villa design (Fig. 3) illustrated in the several editions of Palladio's masterwork that a gentleman of Jacob Ford's position might have owned. Even more compelling evidence is the extraordinarily fine wooden ornament that tempers the simplicity of the main block: the entry and the window above it are decorated with the signature Palladian device, the so-called Palladian window, also known as a Serliana or Venetian window (Fig. 4). An identical Serliana, depicted, like Jacob Ford's, in the Ionic order, appears in *The City and Country Builder's and Workmen's Treasury* by Batty Langley (Fig. 5). Although Langley is only one of several authors that Ford and his master builder might have turned to, the specificity and enriched ornament of the Ionic Serliana they produced point unmistakably to a published design.

Plantation seats and other important houses like those de-

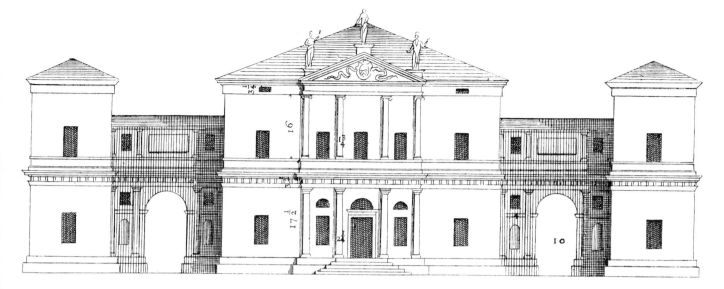

Fig. 3. Carried across two centuries and two continents, Andrea Palladio's designs remained the source for the best colonial American buildings. His Plate XXXV in the second of the Four Books of Architecture *(London, 1738) depicts a villa that might have inspired Jacob Ford's house.*

scribed by the Anglican missionary Thomas Thompson were more numerous in eighteenth-century New Jersey than the small number of surviving examples might lead us to believe. The connection between these houses and their published Palladian sources is easy to see in the evidence that survives. The Jouet house in Elizabeth, now greatly altered, was a rare New Jersey example of a full-blown five-part Palladian villa (Fig. 6) that never could have existed without the inspiration of a published source.

Another Palladian villa, this one recently restored, is the Proprietary House in Perth Amboy, residence of William Franklin, the last royal governor of New Jersey and the natural son of Benjamin Franklin. The scene of splendid levees given by the governor for his Perth Amboy "court," the Proprietary House witnessed one of the most dramatic incidents of the Revolutionary War in New Jersey on January 8, 1776. In William Franklin's own words, "About two o'clock that Night . . . I was awakened with a violent knocking at my Door, which alarmed my wife so much that I was not without Apprehension of her Dying with the Fright. Looking through the Chamber Window I perceived that a Number of armed men had invested the House." Long at odds with his father on political matters, Franklin and his wife, Elizabeth, were placed under house arrest for five months. Exiled in England, the last royal governor received news from a friend in 1784 that carried this sad note:

Fig. 4. The Palladian entry of the Jacob Ford house was drawn in 1935 for the Historic American Buildings Survey.

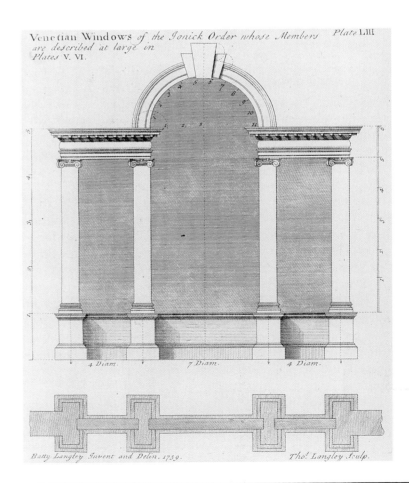

Fig. 5. Plate LIII from Batty Langley's 1750 book, The City and Country Builder's and Workmen's Treasury, *is one of several likely sources for Jacob Ford's Palladian door and window. (Avery Architectural and Fine Arts Library, Columbia University in the City of New York)*

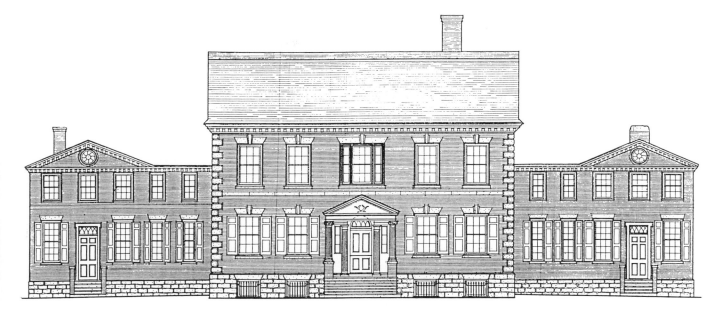

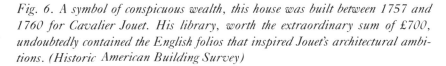

Fig. 6. A symbol of conspicuous wealth, this house was built between 1757 and 1760 for Cavalier Jouet. His library, worth the extraordinary sum of £700, undoubtedly contained the English folios that inspired Jouet's architectural ambitions. (Historic American Building Survey)

"Perth Amboy at present exhibits a scene of Poverty and distress . . . Your House is in a state of ruin, it's declared past repair."[5]

In happier days the Proprietary House had been proclaimed one of the purest Palladian houses in the colonies, grand enough to be called, with some justice, the governor's "palace." Like Jacob Ford's mansion, it once displayed a Serliana window above a matching entry (Fig. 7). Most unusual, the identity of the architect-builder is recorded. John Edward Pryor arrived in America from England in 1761. An accomplished master builder, he was soon commissioned to design several of the most ambitious houses in New York and New Jersey, including the country seat of William Alexander, Lord Stirling, at Basking Ridge. His account books reveal much about the building practice of his time. One striking fact is the brief time he spent on plans for the Proprietary House. The level of detail Pryor produced in such a short time reinforces the belief that folios and builder's books guided his design. We know nothing of the specific sources at his disposal, but his taste was grounded firmly in the precepts of English Palladianism, a fact taken for granted by the well-informed gentlemen he "waited on," who, according to his account book, included "the Earl of Stirling [William Alexander] and Mr. [Robert Hunter] Morris."[6]

Fig. 7. The Proprietary House looked like this when it was the residence of His Excellency William Franklin, Captain General and Governor-in-Chief of the Province of New Jersey. (Model by William Pavlovsky, photographed courtesy of the Proprietary House Association, Perth Amboy, N.J.)

Knowledgeable men like Lord Stirling, Robert Morris, and Jacob Ford were essential to the collaborative effort of patron and master builder that resulted in the best examples of colonial Palladianism. Not only were men of the ruling class educated to believe that architecture was a gentleman's proper pursuit, but they commanded the means to execute their architectural fancies. In a town of rude, unpainted dwellings, imagine the shock of Jacob Ford's new house, with its gleaming white, symmetrical facade enriched with carved classical ornament and abundant window glass reflecting the sunlight—a tangible symbol of its owner's power and taste. Because country seats like Ford's were less numerous in America than they were in England, gentleman-amateurs in New Jersey and throughout the colonies were often compelled to turn to architectural books instead of built examples for their models.

Asher Benjamin and the Federal Style

The ruinous scene described by Governor Franklin's correspondent was familiar in much of post-Revolutionary New Jersey. When conditions improved enough around the turn of the eighteenth century for new construction to flourish, the Georgian style did not vanish overnight. Instead, its bold Palladian aspect gradually changed into a different sort of neoclassicism. Like its Georgian predecessor, high-style Federal architecture was molded by English builders' books. During the Federal period in New Jersey (approximately 1780–1830), the connection between the new architecture and its published sources was found primarily in details. For example, a doorway (Fig. 8) pictured in William Pain's *The Practical Builder* (London, 1774) is the source for innumerable New Jersey entrances. One such high-style doorway graced the entry to the house of the chair maker David Alling in Newark, although the house itself was thoroughly traditional and owed nothing to architectural books (Fig. 9). Not only entrance details but many other features that seem commonplace to us now from a long familiarity with historic buildings were introduced to America by English builders' books during the Federal period. One familiar element is the interlace motif found on cornices. The first published example (Fig. 10) appeared in London in the 1778 edition of *The Practical Builder, or Workman's General Assistant*, another of William Pain's books. A self-proclaimed "Architect and Joiner," Pain wrote seven builders' books. All were notable for their clear illustrations of details, and all were influential in America.

Public buildings as well as dwellings benefited from Pain's published designs. The Presbyterian Church in Springfield, dating from 1791, displays Pain's interlace on its prominent cornice (Fig. 11); so does the First Presbyterian Church in Elizabeth, 1784–1786. Although both were built to replace churches burned by the English during the Revolution, the congregations and their builders relied on English architectural taste, just as they had before the war. The anonymous master builders responsible for these commissions had only English books to turn to.

The dominance of English architectural books began to change thanks to the work of one man, Asher Benjamin (1771–1845), who is credited with writing the first American architectural handbook, *The Country Builder's Assistant*, published in 1797. Although Benjamin acknowledged his reliance on English authors William Pain and Sir William Chambers, he established an important precedent for American architectural publishing and encouraged the movement from Palladianism to a native American interpretation of the refined neoclassicism that was being practiced in Great Britain by Robert and James Adam. Enormously influential though they were, Benjamin's books rarely resulted in line-for-line copies. Instead, the details and facades he proposed found their way into the mainstream of New Jersey vernacular building. We know, for example, that one early-nineteenth-century New Jersey–born carpenter named Elias Beach owned Benjamin's *The American Builder's Companion* (Fig. 12), a book so widely used that it ran to six edi-

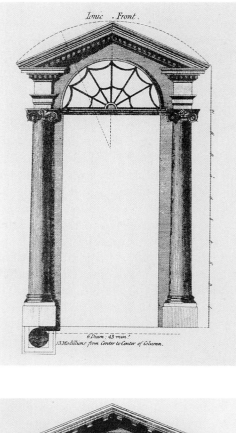

Fig. 8. The 1774 edition of William Pain's The Practical Builder *contained these influential illustrations of doorways based on the classical orders. (Avery Architectural and Fine Arts Library, Columbia University in the City of New York)*

tions between 1806 and 1827. A plan and a facade drawing (Fig. 13) found folded into Beach's copy of the book, now owned by the Newark Public Library, are indebted to Benjamin's designs. They illustrate the direct connection between published sources and the working methods of a carpenter-builder like Beach.

One house where Asher Benjamin's influence can be seen clearly is Edward Sharp's, in Camden (Fig. 14). Completed in 1812, it owes its overall composition and many of its features to Plate 51 in the 1806 edition of *The American Builder's Companion*. The belt course, severe facade, and round-arched entry come directly from Benjamin's design (Fig. 15), but the differences in the house as built are every bit as significant as the similarities to the published design. Most important, the builder dispensed with Benjamin's third floor and raised basement. The deletion of the top story may have been for economy's sake only, but the lack of a high basement is found consistently in New Jersey buildings of this period that are adapted from published sources. Its absence is probably due to a strong vernacular tradition, which produced

Fig. 9. The House and Shop of David Alling *was painted by an unidentified artist about 1835. He recorded a typical combination of a traditional dwelling embellished with a high-style doorway. (Collections of the New Jersey Historical Society, Newark, N.J., gift of Mrs. Clarence Willis Alling)*

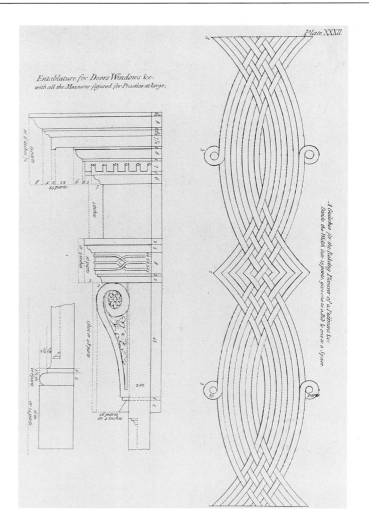

Fig. 10. William Pain's 1778 depiction marks the first publication of the interlace motif, adopted widely in post–Revolutionary War America. (Avery Architectural and Fine Arts Library, Columbia University in the City of New York)

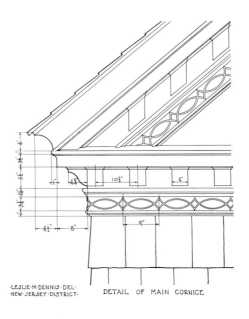

Fig. 11. The interlace motif decorates the cornice of the First Presbyterian Church of Springfield, built in 1791. (Historic American Buildings Survey)

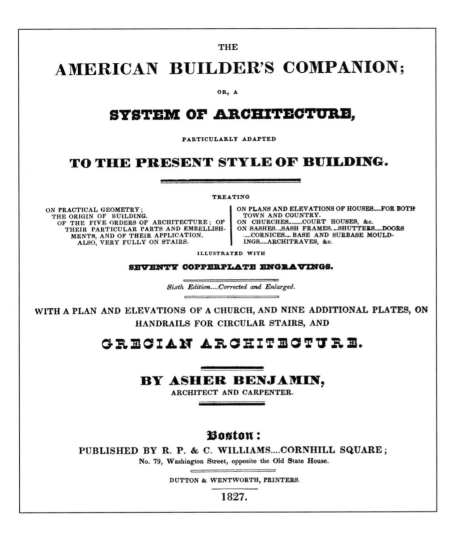

THE

AMERICAN BUILDER'S COMPANION;

OR, A

SYSTEM OF ARCHITECTURE,

PARTICULARLY ADAPTED

TO THE PRESENT STYLE OF BUILDING.

TREATING

| ON PRACTICAL GEOMETRY; THE ORIGIN OF BUILDING. OF THE FIVE ORDERS OF ARCHITECTURE; OF THEIR PARTICULAR PARTS AND EMBELLISH-MENTS, AND OF THEIR APPLICATION. ALSO, VERY FULLY ON STAIRS. | ON PLANS AND ELEVATIONS OF HOUSES....FOR BOTH TOWN AND COUNTRY. ON CHURCHES........COURT HOUSES, &c. ON SASHES...SASH FRAMES...SHUTTERS.....DOORS ....CORNICES... BASE AND SURBASE MOULD-INGS.....ARCHITRAVES, &c. |

ILLUSTRATED WITH

SEVENTY COPPERPLATE ENGRAVINGS.

Sixth Edition....Corrected and Enlarged.

WITH A PLAN AND ELEVATIONS OF A CHURCH, AND NINE ADDITIONAL PLATES, ON HANDRAILS FOR CIRCULAR STAIRS, AND

GRECIAN ARCHITECTURE.

BY ASHER BENJAMIN,

ARCHITECT AND CARPENTER.

Boston:

PUBLISHED BY R. P. & C. WILLIAMS....CORNHILL SQUARE;

No. 79, Washington Street, opposite the Old State House.

DUTTON & WENTWORTH, PRINTERS.

1827.

Fig. 12. Asher Benjamin's best-known build-ers' handbook guided the work of American carpenters for well over a quarter-century.

ground-hugging houses that carpenter-builders were reluctant to abandon. The result is a slightly less high-style house than Benjamin intended, but one that illustrates the freedom with which New Jersey builders and their clients used architectural books.

A simple townhouse like Edward Sharp's, often built as one of several units to form an urban row, became a familiar sight in the years following the first edition of *The American Builder's Companion*. By contrast, most freestanding country seats of the same era in New Jersey were conservative five-bay rectangular blocks that had evolved directly out of the Georgian tradition, even though updated with lighter proportions and more delicate Federal details. A few elaborate houses were built for more ambitious and affluent owners. One of the most unusual is "Fenwick Manor" in New Lisbon, Pemberton Township, in the Pine Barrens (Fig. 16). Not a simple rectangle by any standard, Fenwick Manor eschews the horizontal emphasis of the familiar five-bay center-hall house in

Fig. 13. A plan and elevation found folded into Elias Beach's copy of The American Builder's Companion *shows how an early-nineteenth-century builder used published sources. (Newark Public Library)*

Fig. 14. The restraint typical of Federal architecture is apparent in the severe facade of Edward Sharp's Camden house.

Fig. 15. Plate 51 from the first edition of The American Builder's Companion *depicts a planar facade, prominent belt course, and round-arched entry—all features of the Edward Sharp house.*

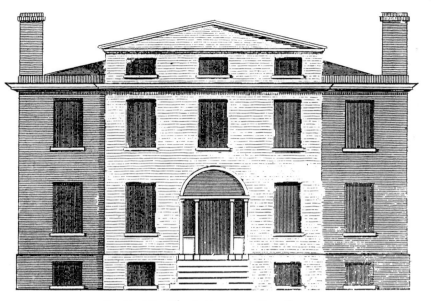

Plate 55.

Scale 15 Feet to one Inch

Fig. 17. Plate 55 from The American Builder's Companion *is clearly the inspiration for Fenwick Manor.*

favor of a vertical composition distinguished by a gabled and pedimented facade. These unusually high-style features are taken, appropriately enough, from "Designs for a House Intended for the Country," Plate 55 in the sixth edition of *The American Builder's Companion* (Fig. 17).

Typical of many pattern-book translations of the era, Fenwick Manor was built with several design adjustments. Instead of Benjamin's high basement, the New Lisbon version, like Edward Sharp's house in Camden, is raised only slightly above ground level (the porch is a later addition), but its center section includes a full third floor, not merely an attic. The facade is graced with a lunette window, Ionic pilasters, and cornices defined by classical moldings. These enrichments cannot be found on Benjamin's typically schematic elevation drawing, but all of them appear as details elsewhere in the same book.

What kind of owner could afford the high-style extravagance of Fenwick Manor? Benjamin Jones, who bought land for a country estate in 1827—the very year that saw the last edition of *The American Builder's Companion*—was one of the foremost ironmasters in

Fig. 16. (opposite) The front-facing pedimented gable of Fenwick Manor is a feature rarely found in New Jersey's Federal-era architecture.

the Pinelands; his chief source of wealth was the Hanover Furnace. Soon after acquiring the property, Jones built the Columbus, Kinkora, and Springfield Railroad, designed to haul the products of his forges, which included huge shipments of pipe for the Philadelphia Waterworks.[7] His Philadelphia connections undoubtedly contributed to his architectural sophistication. His proximity to such a cosmopolitan center notwithstanding, it is significant that Jones turned to a pattern book and not to an architect to realize his building ambitions.

As an example of up-to-date Federal design, Fenwick Manor displays unusual fidelity to its published model. More typical was a free approach to architectural handbooks that continued to characterize New Jersey building at least through the first third of the nineteenth century, when builders combined Georgian and Federal

Fig. 18. Morris County Courthouse, 1827, from an old engraving.

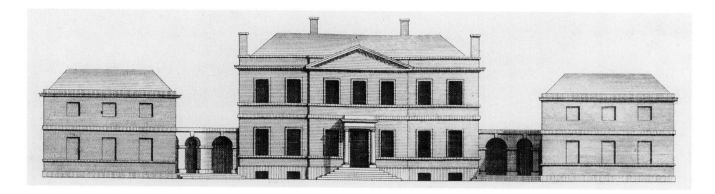

aspects of neoclassicism, with hybridized results. A good idea of how this process worked can be deduced from an examination of the Morris County Courthouse in Morristown (Fig. 18).

Completed in 1827, the courthouse was constructed and presumably designed by two carpenter-builders of local repute, Joseph M. Lindsley and Lewis Carter. The new courthouse, sited just off the Morristown Green, was a symbol of justice and civic rectitude, and, after the nearby Presbyterian Church, it was the most imposing building in town. How did Lindsley and Carter arrive at a design for such an important building? By separating the courthouse into its constituent parts, we can gain some insight into their probable

Fig. 19. The central block of a Palladian-inspired villa published in A Book of Architecture *by James Gibbs in 1728 is nearly identical to the Morris County Courthouse. (Avery Architectural and Fine Arts Library, Columbia University in the City of New York)*

Fig. 20. Morris County Courthouse with its cupola erased for comparative purposes.

Fig. 21. Plate 58 from The American Builder's Companion *depicts a courthouse that could have been another source of inspiration for Carter and Lindsley's courthouse in Morristown.*

methods. We should remember that most public buildings in early nineteenth-century New Jersey were very like the best private dwellings in size and scale. With this fact in mind, it is easy to see the correspondence between the facade of the courthouse and a villa, or country house, depicted in *A Book of Architecture* by James Gibbs, first published in London in 1728 (Fig. 19). By blotting out the cupola on a nineteenth-century engraving of the courthouse, the resemblance between the two becomes unmistakable (Fig. 20).

Lindsley and Carter might have composed their cupola with the help of any number of sources. Sir William Chambers's *Treatise on Civil Architecture* was published in 1759, but conservative American builders were still making reference to it more than half a century later. One of its unnumbered plates, identifiable by its dedication to John Hall Stevenson, depicts a tiny domed building with its corners defined by columns positioned in the same manner as those on the courthouse cupola. The combination of Palladio's villa block with the domed and columned "tempietto" from Chambers brings us very close to the Morris County Courthouse, but something is still missing.

Would Lindsley and Carter have owned a copy of Asher Benjamin's *The American Builder's Companion?* Most likely they would have, in light of its wide currency for more than twenty years. Referring to Plate 58 in the 1827 edition (Fig. 21), they would have found a courthouse design that featured an Ionic-columned center pavilion. By divesting that design of its monumental ground floor and visualizing Benjamin's Ionic order superimposed on the more domestically scaled facade of Palladio's villa (with Chambers's cupola added!), we at last arrive at a design strikingly similar to that of the courthouse in Morristown. The process of selection and combination sounds tortuous in the telling. In practice, it was second nature to generations of builders who learned their published sources almost by heart.

Lindsley and Carter's debt to English Palladianism was certainly old-fashioned by 1827, but books like Benjamin's would have helped them combine the venerable, Georgian kind of neoclassicism with the newer architectural outlook. Asher Benjamin's delineation of Federal-style neoclassicism emphasized its lightness and its linearity, and the delicate character of its ornament. His simplified drawings of building facades ("elevations") helped give wide currency to a number of features that Lindsley and Carter used for their courthouse design, such as tall, round-arched windows, delicate, leaded window tracery, and attenuated, or stretched-out, columns. Their combination of Georgian and Federal motifs is both retardataire and ingenious, a demonstration of how skilled but conservative carpenter-builders were able to combine material from published sources with their knowledge of local building practice to produce harmonious and original results.

Minard Lafever and the Greek Revival

The designs in Asher Benjamin's early books contributed to the uniform and refined appearance of New Jersey architecture during the Federal period, but by the 1830s Benjamin had begun to advocate another way of designing from classical sources, a revival and adaptation of ancient Greek prototypes. The same neoclassical spirit that had informed Georgian and Federal architecture, essentially English styles even in America, reemerged with fresh vigor in its new Greek guise. This enthusiasm for a new architecture came at a time when New Jerseyans could afford to build new houses. Across the state, improved transportation spurred economic growth. Like its old architecture, the state's old turnpikes no longer met modern needs. Construction began on the Delaware and Raritan Canal in 1832, the same year that the Morris Canal opened. The Morris and Essex Railroad first steamed through Morristown in 1837, just six years after the Camden and Amboy Railroad, the first in New Jersey and the second in the United States, was inaugurated. It is little wonder, then, that in 1831 Alexis de Tocqueville observed:

I was surprised to perceive along the shore, at some distance from the city, a considerable number of little palaces of white marble, several of which were built after the models of ancient architecture. When I went next day to inspect more closely the building which had particularly attracted my notice, I found that its walls were of white-washed brick and its columns of painted wood. All of the edifices that I had admired the night before were of the same kind.[8]

Tocqueville was describing New York City, but across the Hudson River in New Jersey this same combination of lofty classical aspirations rendered in humble materials was typical of the search for a new style. At first American builders were influenced by European models: Russia, the Scandinavian countries, Germany, England, and Scotland (most particularly Edinburgh) had shown enthusiasm for neoclassical architecture based explicitly on Greek precedents as early as the end of the eighteenth century, when archaeological campaigns were bringing to light new facts about the ancient world. Almost immediately, however, the American response to these classical cues assumed its own distinctive flavor.

Much has been written about American infatuation with the political ideals of ancient Greece, supposedly another spur to the creation of "Grecian" buildings, but some recent scholarship seeks to minimize this theory. Roger G. Kennedy, in *Greek Revival America*, argues in favor of broad cultural influences rather than political emulation. The word "classic," in early-nineteenth-century America, claims Kennedy, stood for qualities like simplicity, austerity, and heroism, and it was these the young republic sought to translate into wood and brick. Contemporaneous with the admiration of classical virtues was the American Academy movement, which promoted education based on the classical verities. In George Macculloch's Latin Academy in Morristown, young scholars became familiar with classical language and literature—and Macculloch Hall eventually acquired a massive Greek portico; as late as the middle of the nineteenth century, Mendham's newly arrived Presbyterian minister was astonished to hear the local farmers quoting Latin and Greek.[9] American enthusiasm for Greek architecture becomes more comprehensible in light of this classical inheritance common to all literate citizens.

Although Asher Benjamin had embraced the new way of building, it was a younger man who helped to push Greek Revival architecture squarely into the limelight, giving it the same cachet that Benjamin had given the Federal style. Born near Morristown, Minard Lafever (1798–1854) moved to the Finger Lakes region of New York while still a child. As a young man, he became a carpenter and in 1824 took up residence in New York City. Five years later he published his first book, *The Young Builder's General Instructor*, in Newark, New Jersey. Like his late-Federal predecessors, Lafever focused on technical information, and in that sense his book was still very much a handbook rather than a pattern book, a work designed for carpenters rather than for householders searching for a house design. In Lafever's own words, it was concerned with "geometry as connected with practical carpentry, veneering, arches and groins, niches, coverings of polygonal and hemispherical roofs, pendentives, domes, circular sashes and hand-railing." More significantly, Lafever provided his readers with rules for the accurate proportioning and ornamentation of the Doric, Ionic, and Corinthian orders, the basis of ancient Greek architecture. The carpenter-builders who used Lafever's book expected to create houses based on their own understanding of the classical design vocabulary, so complete house designs remained a negligible aspect of Greek Revival architectural books. For that reason, we find few direct matches among examples built during this period.

Even when filtered through the powerful vernacular tradition that continued to dominate New Jersey building throughout the first four decades of the nineteenth century, Greek Revival architecture could not have existed without the influence of printed sources. A good example of the creative tension and compromise between published designs and local traditions is the Major Aaron Hudson house in Mendham. Aaron Hudson (1801–1888) was a prolific carpenter-builder, who by the time of the 1850 census was called "architect." We know nothing about his training, but the surviving buildings that can be ascribed to him with certainty prove that he was adept at both the Greek and the Gothic Revival styles. His own house (Fig. 22) illustrates the kind of dwelling that a forward-thinking and talented man in a small New Jersey town viewed as up-to-date in 1840. It is precisely the kind of modestly pretentious dwelling that the Greek style made possible, its break with tradition announced by a pedimented portico pushed beyond the facade as an almost-freestanding element. Meant to recall the front of an ancient temple, this bold device is emblematic of the Greek Revival style. How Hudson used the pedimented portico and other typical motifs tells us how devoutly he adhered to published sources and how free he felt to take liberties with them.

If we look at the frontispiece (Fig. 23) from Minard Lafever's second book, *The Modern Builder's Guide*, we see a design that must have struck the young Aaron Hudson with its novelty and forcefulness if he saw it when it first appeared in 1833. Titled "Design for a Country Villa," it features the same pedimented portico carried on four square piers that Hudson would adopt seven years later. But instead of imitating the two-story block flanked by lower wings, Hudson grafted Lafever's portico to his own version of the venerable Georgian-Federal house with five bays and a center hall,

Fig. 22. The up-to-date pediment of Aaron Hudson's house is joined to a traditional five-bay dwelling. Its debt to Minard Lafever's work is strong nonetheless.

a fact not apparent at first because of the way the portico dominates the otherwise traditional facade. As if to compensate for his conservatism, he decorated the facade with pilasters and an entablature and covered the three-bay center section with flush boards to mimic dressed stone, a contrast to the traditional clapboard that sheathes the rest of the house.

Aaron Hudson's neighbors might have been puzzled by this reminiscence of ancient Greece set down in their collective dooryard, but Hudson's house is an important transitional building for New Jersey. Though still rooted firmly in an earlier, vernacular tradition that would persist for another generation, it nonetheless turns a new and influential face on the architectural scene. The force of its newness is concentrated in one element, the pedimented portico that serves as architectural shorthand to suggest an entire Greek temple. The pediment would be repeated countless times in the 1840s and 1850s, mostly in the northern and central parts of the state. The combination of pediment with the square pillars depicted by Lafever was appealing to many New Jersey builders, possibly for a reason Lafever had not intended: economy. Pillars, or square columns, were simply cheaper and easier to build than classical columns. The same kind of two-story (or "colossal") piers found in Mendham supported a pedimented portico at the

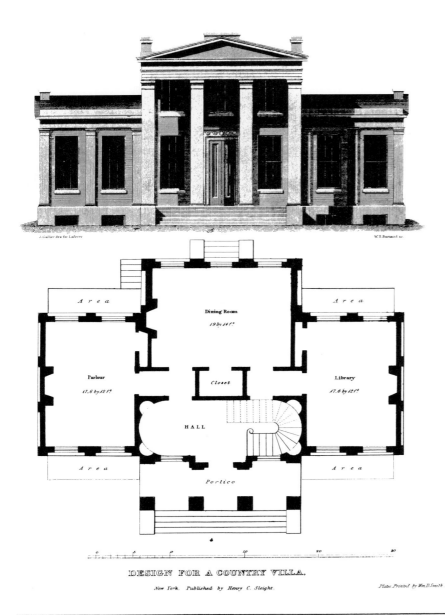

Fig. 23. *The one-story flanking wings and authentically shallow pediment are two of the features that distinguish Lafever's "Design for a Country Villa" from the Hudson house, its vernacular offspring.*

SECOND FL. CEILING

SECOND FLOOR

FIRST FL. CEILING

FIRST FLOOR

BASEMENT FLOOR

CLAP BOARDS

WOOD LATTICE BRICK

BRICK

CLAPBOARDS

GRADE

SOUTH-WEST ELEVATION

Fig. 24. The Lufbery homestead in Rahway is a Greek Revival interpretation of a traditional New Jersey house type. John O. Lufbery's prosperity was based on a lumber business and nail manufactury, established about 1827. (Historic American Buildings Survey)

Lufbery Homestead (now destroyed) in Rahway (Fig. 24). It is another traditional house in Greek dress, in this case built on a three-bay side-hall plan with a two-bay wing instead of a five-bay center-hall plan like Aaron Hudson's.

By the 1840s Greek Revival pattern books were influential enough to have two kinds of impact on New Jersey builders: the creation of new dwellings and the remodeling of older houses. A striking example of the latter practice can be found in Morristown. Between 1810 and 1814, George and Louisa Macculloch built for themselves three successive wings of what became an imposing but decidedly vernacular brick Federal house, with a Latin Academy in the final wing. The Macculloch family (seven grandchildren were raised in Macculloch Hall, or "The Old House," as it came to be known) and the Latin Academy's boarding students justified such a large house, but oddly enough for a man of George Macculloch's means and prestige (he was the visionary who conceived the idea of the Morris Canal and promoted its construction), the exterior of his house was architecturally plain to the point of bareness.

Several decades after the Academy wing was completed, someone decided to improve the severe, barracks-like facade of Macculloch Hall. This final building campaign took the form of a huge pedimented portico (Fig. 25), with dramatic results: for the first time the endless facade was graced with a powerful focal point. Although the voluminous Macculloch family records fail to docu-

Fig. 25. The portico of Macculloch Hall, Morristown, is classical architecture reduced to its most basic form.

ment the portico—whose idea it might have been or precisely when it was added—its break with the architecture of the Federal era illustrates the power of the new Greek attitude toward classical forms and the importance of the new pattern books that promoted it. Once again Lafever's "Design for a Country Villa" seems to have been the most likely source for this simplest of porticos, with its four boxlike pillars instead of classical columns.

We find pillars used not only to make otherwise traditional houses speak Greek but also on houses with decidedly high-style aspirations. "Boisaubin" in Chatham Township incorporates four square pillars as part of its tetrastyle portico (Fig. 26). Built for the French émigré Vincent Boisaubin (probably by local housewright W. M. Kitchell), it is an assertive house that points toward the mature phase of the Greek Revival style. The house itself is nearly cubical, so that its pedimented portico stands out beyond the facade like an independent temple, precisely the effect that builders and owners of the day were seeking. The high-style identity of Boisaubin is further enhanced by the large scale of its rooms and their simple but effective Greek Revival window and door frames, unlike anything seen in Georgian or Federal houses. The dimensions of the center hall (13′6″ wide with a 12′6″ ceiling) give some idea of the designer's generous hand. Biographical information about Vincent Boisaubin suggests that his house was built about 1834 or soon thereafter. When we remember that Lafever's first mature Greek Revival pattern book appeared in 1833, the likely connection between house and book becomes apparent.

Although the national emergence of the Greek Revival style is generally dated at 1818 with William Strickland's Second Bank of the United States in Philadelphia, it arrived late in many parts of New Jersey, especially in rural areas. Moreover, it persisted into the 1850s and even the 1860s, to challenge the early ascendency of the Italianate and Gothic Revival styles. As late as 1854, when William Ranlett published *The Architect*, he included a design for a "Grecian Cottage" that is unlike the temple-front pedimented houses favored by Lafever and others in the 1830s (Fig. 27). It is most patently Greek by virtue of its columns of the Ionic order. The hip-roofed, five-bay house with low attic concealing a full second floor is an uncommon Greek Revival type in New Jersey. Ranlett noted that it was built "on the banks of the Passaic River" in Lodi, but evidence exists that at least one prosperous farmer in another part of the state saw and was impressed by the design.

In 1830 Jacob Wise Neighbor bought half of his father's homestead farm in Washington Township. He must have managed his land well, because in 1850, when he was forty-five years old, the United States Census made it clear that he had become one of the wealthiest men of his generation in German Valley, today's Long Valley. The census taker noted that Jacob and his wife, Mary, had

Fig. 26. Boisaubin, in Chatham Township, is proof that even a highly sophisti-
cated Greek Revival house might rely on Minard Lafever's pillared rather than
columned temple-front design.

three daughters and four sons, reason enough to build a large, new
house (Fig. 28). Unlike any other in the neighborhood, it is a simplified version of Ranlett's sophisticated cottage. Instead of six
Ionic columns, its porch is carried on six square Tuscan pillars, but
the porch cornice and main cornice display full entablatures, and
five "attic" or frieze-band windows are found in the upper story,
all elements of the same distinctive treatment that Ranlett pictured. His published ground-floor dimensions match those of the
house Jacob Neighbor built, and his description of an elaborate
dairy room in the basement was also followed by Neighbor. The

most telling connection, however, is the lantern or cupola in Ranlett's plate. Today, Jacob and Mary's house has none—but it once did. A scarred second-floor ceiling is unmistakable proof that the low bedroom story was once lighted by just such a feature.

The short time that elapsed between the publication of Ranlett's book and the probable construction date of the Neighbor house is typical of how many pattern-book-derived houses were built in New Jersey: soon after seeing a new design in print, a property owner would have it built to satisfy his desire for an up-to-date residence that symbolized good taste and economic good fortune. In the case of the Neighbor house, the result proves that printed sources made high-style Greek Revival architecture of notable refinement and craftsmanship available, if not widespread, in New Jersey as late as the 1850s.

Although buildings intended for public assembly mostly lie outside the scope of this book, no discussion of the Greek Revival can ignore its influence on churches and courthouses. A list of New Jersey churches in the Grecian mode would include typical examples in Basking Ridge, Colt's Neck, New Brunswick, Rocky Hill, Chester, Griggstown, Princeton, and Mount Olive, but their number is nearly endless. Most are distinguished by porticoed temple-front facades based on the classical orders illustrated by Asher Benjamin and Minard Lafever. One building that might stand as symbolic of this whole class of courthouses and churches is the Middlesex County Courthouse of 1841 (Fig. 29).

As early as 1826 the Middlesex County Freeholders began to discuss the need for a new seat of justice in New Brunswick. The movement gained fresh impetus when "the Chief Justice in his charge to the Grand Inquest, at the June term, 1835, [commented] on the want of a suitable building as a public grievance."[10] After further delays and visits by a building committee to courthouses in New Jersey and New York, a design was approved in 1838. "Mr. Lafevre, the architect who prepared the draft and plan, very frankly stated that if called on to prepare another plan, he did not think it possible to suggest any improvement."[11] The "unimprovable" building was a hexastyle, or six-columned, temple-front block designed on the Doric order, a dignified edifice intended to express judicial dignity and thus bound to satisfy the demanding chief justice.

Mr. Lefevre (one of several family spellings), its architect, was named Minard, but he was not the Minard Lafever whose acquaintance we have made already. The Middlesex Minard was a first cousin of the famous architect-author, to whom he had been apprenticed.[12] It is not suprising, therefore, that the courthouse should display a monumental simplicity and a degree of historical accuracy in individual details like its Doric entablature that were a direct result of Minard Lafever's books (Fig. 30).

RICHARDSON. SC.

Fig. 27. William Ranlett's "Design for a Grecian Cottage" is an uncommon interpretation of the style in New Jersey. (Avery Architectural and Fine Arts Library, Columbia University in the City of New York)

Fig. 28. Now shorn of its cupola, the Jacob W. Neighbor house in Washington Township still exhibits other prominent features that correspond to William Ranlett's pattern-book design.

Fig. 29. The Greek Doric order was the design basis for the Middlesex County Courthouse, dedicated in 1839. Unusually long-lived for an American public building, it survived for ninety-nine years. (Special Collection and Archives, Rutgers University Libraries)

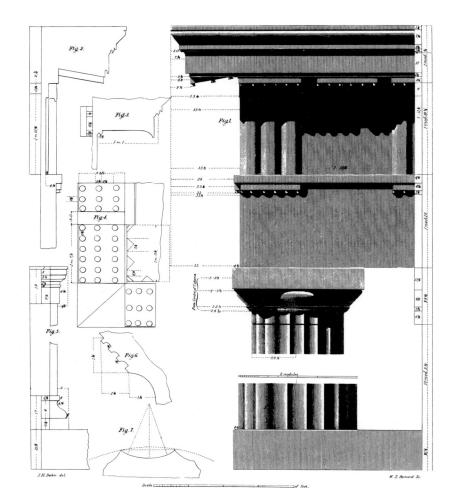

Fig. 30. The Doric order was the subject of Plate 46 in The Modern Builder's Guide. The beauty and clarity of Lafever's illustrations promoted the Greek Revival style for both public and private buildings.

Versatility was the most striking fact about the vocabulary of Greek elements that local builders learned to use from books. The way they combined historical features may rarely have been correct archaeologically, but the columns, pediments, entablatures, and door enframents with which these country and city carpenters grew familiar imparted grace and dignity to many otherwise simple New Jersey houses. In fact they were applied with far greater frequency to simple houses than they were to the important but numerically fewer Greek Revival churches and courthouses. The pedimented or fully temple-fronted facades we have seen were always in the minority in New Jersey. More representative is the small portico of the James Townley house on the Kean College campus in Union (Fig. 31). The original house was built before 1796 and was later modernized in the Grecian mode. Although its columns are, by classical tenets, incorrectly attenuated, the bold Doric entablature

Fig. 31. The James Townley house in Union represents an entire class of dwellings that were Greek Revival by virtue of little more than classical porticos.

they support is accurate enough in its scale and detailing to suggest that the carpenter-builder who designed it must have turned to a pattern book for guidance.

In all of New Jersey the most consistent and pleasing Greek Revival environment created under the influence of pattern books is found in Princeton, where, in the 1830s and 1840s, one man produced some seventy buildings of unusual uniformity and competence. Charles Steadman "was a typical carpenter-builder. Beginning as a carpenter working in the traditional methods of his time, he went on to become a self-taught builder-architect, basing the designs for his buildings on a combination of his own practical

Fig. 32. View of Alexander Street, Princeton, where a host of Greek Revival details adds up to a powerful whole.

knowledge and ideas he . . . derived from the pattern books of architects such as Minard Lafever or Asher Benjamin."[13]

In some ways the most noteworthy of Steadman's surviving creations are sections of Alexander and Mercer streets, where a collection of two-story frame houses, most with modest, columned porticoes, illustrates his fusion of elegant Greek details with a conservative house type (Fig. 32). These details result in a powerful urbanistic impression when viewed together. Direct pattern-book matches are sometimes apparent. The house at 112 Mercer Street (home to Albert Einstein during his years at Princeton University, 1932 to 1955) was designed not by Steadman himself but by a contemporary named Samuel Stevens (Fig. 33). Its entryway pilasters are taken from Plate XXVIII (Fig. 34) in Asher Benjamin's *The Architect*, published in 1830, just a few years before the Princeton doorway was created.

Although Charles Steadman continued to design into the early 1860s, his originality had faded by then, just as enthusiasm for the Greek Revival had been extinguished in most of New Jersey by the end of the 1850s. Theodore Dwight, writing in 1834, when the style was fresh, could exclaim, "How much more appropriate are the pure and chaste Greek styles to our own history, character and condition!"[14] But by 1852 many Americans had come to agree with a London observer writing in *The Builder*, who expressed nothing but contempt for what some had embraced as a national style:

> The Americans seem to be affected by an absolute mania for Greek temples, or what will look like such at first glance, or seem from the distance. Public and private buildings are all dressed up and disguised in that uniform, and the greater part in a bungling manner . . . so preposterously has that style been taken up, without any regard to principle or character, as to be rendered anything but classical, one in which columns alone give the architectural expression.[15]

The Englishman was both right and wrong. As the work of Charles Steadman amply illustrates, carefully conceived details like columns, although certainly not columns alone, did give American Greek Revival architecture much of its animation, and many builder-architects learned to design and combine such details with the help of pattern books like Benjamin's and Lafever's. When he complained that American Greek Revival architecture had been "rendered anything but classical," the English critic unwittingly hit upon a central truth. If the Greek Revival style was little better than naively misunderstood classicism in the eyes of a transatlantic observer, it was also the logical culmination of more than a century of American *neo*classicism that had evolved from Georgian through Federal to Greek. And if the Greek Revival

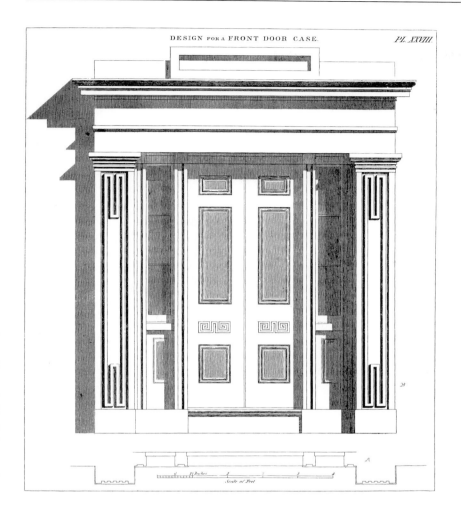

DESIGN FOR A FRONT DOOR CASE.   PL. XXVIII.

Fig. 34. Plate XXVIII from The Architect *illustrates Asher Benjamin's evolution from the delicate ornament of the Federal style to the solid geometrical emphasis of the Greek Revival.*

represented the last of neoclassicism (at least for a time), it was, simultaneously, the genesis of a new outlook in American architecture, a new Romantic way of looking at the built world that would soon become "anything but classical."

Just as architectural books had developed and changed along with neoclassicism, they were about to play an even larger role in propagating the new Romantic taste. As the curtain fell on the era of the Greek Revival, more Americans than ever needed new houses and could command the economic means to build them in the latest fashion. Architectural books were about to fulfill those needs as they exploded into their period of greatest importance.

Fig. 33. (opposite) The angular pilaster ornament at the entrance to this house on Mercer Street in Princeton comes directly from a late book by Asher Benjamin, The Architect, *1830.*

Georgian Interiors

The architectural folios and builders' books of the eighteenth century included details of stairways, chimneypieces, and moldings, but rarely provided complete floor plans. The creation of interiors, like exteriors, depended on a skilled carpenter who could assemble various parts of the classical language into a coherent whole. By the middle of the eighteenth century there was consensus, at least among English-speaking colonists, about what a proper interior should include. A hall was required, containing exterior doors and stairs to the upper floor. Two rooms, back to back, entered by separate hall doors, constituted the side-hall house. With a symmetrical arrangement of two rooms on either side of the hall, the center-hall Georgian ideal was achieved (Fig. 35).

Rooms were cubical in feeling if not in precise dimensions, and strict symmetry ordered the placement of windows and doors. The practical Georgian side-hall and center-hall plans later served as the base for the decorative embellishments of Federal and Greek Revival interiors.

The best Georgian interiors displayed details copied directly from English architectural books. Two well-known examples are Mount Vernon and the Jeremiah Lee house in Marblehead, Massachusetts, both with mantels taken from Abraham Swan's *The British Architect*. Few examples of such direct building by the book have been documented for eighteenth-century New Jersey, but the influence of published sources on grand New Jersey interiors is strong

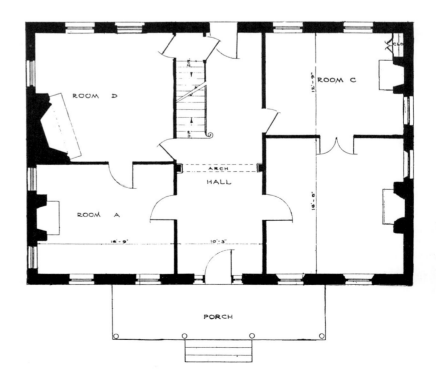

Fig. 35. Center-hall plan, adapted from Historic American Buildings Survey plan of the Tilton house, Walnford, New Jersey.

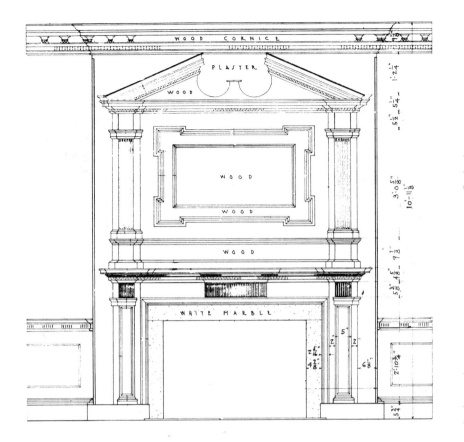

Fig. 36. Drawing of parlor mantel from the Imlay mansion, Allentown, New Jersey. (Historic American Buildings Survey)

Fig. 37. Plate 23 from Abraham Swan's Designs in Architecture, 1757. (Avery Architectural and Fine Arts Library, Columbia University in the City of New York)

nonetheless. Another of Abraham Swan's books, *Designs in Architecture*, published in 1757, is a likely source for parts of at least two important interiors. The Imlay mansion, built about 1790 in Allentown, features a gorgeous parlor mantel with elaborate overmantel (Fig. 36). Its broken pediment and interior frame with shouldered corners resemble Swan's Plate 23 (Fig. 37), although the mantelpiece proper is quite different. At "Pomona Hall" in Camden, the original house of 1728 was remodeled with some high-style elements in 1788. In the dining room one wall incorporates a boldly simple mantelpiece with shouldered architrave below a paneled overmantel wall with shouldered corners (Fig. 38). Swan's Plate 21 could have provided the basis for this combination of details (Fig. 39).

The Proprietary House in Perth Amboy was built in the 1760s as the Royal Governor's residence. The original interior is gone, but contemporary accounts describe wainscot and cornices, and ceilings with elaborate plaster ornament, all of a kind that would have been designed with folios and builders' books in hand. Ample documentation of the original decoration survives, in Governor William Franklin's own hand. Franklin followed the mid-eighteenth-century fashion for decorating rooms with paint, wallpaper, upholstery, and window hangings of a single color. His sketched floor plan shows that the drawing room was "to be papered with a handsome Yellow Paper suitable for [i.e., compatible with] Yellow Silk Damask Curtains, Chairs, etc." The dining room was to be red and white, and Franklin's study, green. The walls of "Governor and Mrs. F.'s Bed Chamber" were "blue & white striped, of a particular pattern, sent for to England by Captain All."[16]

It was the royal governor himself, and not his lady, who made these choices. Just as gentlemen were expected to know something about architecture, decorating was a man's province as well. William Alexander, Lord Stirling, was a Proprietor of East Jersey at the time Franklin was governor. "The Buildings," his country seat near Basking Ridge in Somerset County, may have been New Jersey's most opulent plantation. Like the governor, Lord Stirling personally supervised the decoration of his domain, and like the Proprietary House, The Buildings had single-color rooms, as can be deduced from a bill for:

> "Putting up a Yellow Check Bed
> Putting up three suites of Crimson Silk Window curtains
> Ditto Green bed and window curtains
> Ditto Blue Calico."[17]

There is little doubt that most eighteenth-century New Jerseyans did not decorate at all. The hard work needed to put food on their tables and clothes on their backs did not admit of the time

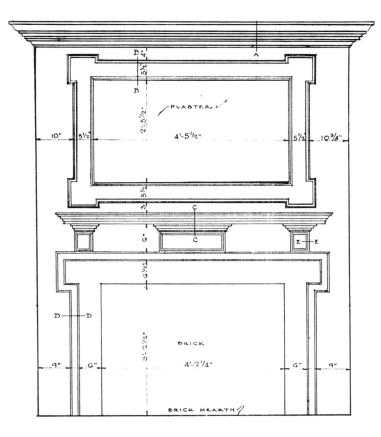

Fig. 38. Drawing of mantel in southwest room, first floor, Pomona Hall, Camden. (Historic American Buildings Survey)

Fig. 39. Plate 21 from Abraham Swan's Designs in Architecture, 1757. *(Avery Architectural and Fine Arts Library, Columbia University in the City of New York)*

and money needed to ponder the merits of yellow silk over crimson damask. Still, the decorative touches found on modest pieces of furniture, household objects, and textiles prove that the decorative impulse was irrepressible.

By the early nineteenth century growing prosperity and the mass production of once-luxury items like wallpaper began to bring interior decorating to a whole new class of people and houses. In 1807, Stephen Youngs of Hanover Township recorded the following tasks in his memorandum book:

> JANUARY 8: *Friday I worked at papering my room, had William Addison to help me. We put all the papering on except the bordering.*
> JANUARY 10: *We put on the bordering until one o'clock then adjourned until evening.*
> JANUARY 12: *I worked at making five boards and covering them with paper for my two front rooms & making window curtains, &c.*
> JANUARY 14: *I carted some timber and painted my front bedroom over.*[18]

Stephen Youngs, carpenter and farmer, not only built his family's house, but decorated it as well. He continued to make notes in his daybook about repainting rooms, and in 1817 recorded a trip to Morristown to buy Prussian blue for his "Dwelling Room." There was no further mention of making curtains, however.

The First American Builders' Books

Before the appearance of Asher Benjamin's *The Country Builder's Assistant* in 1797, a few English builders' books and architectural treatises had been reissued in pirated editions by enterprising printers in Boston and Philadelphia. But the growing confidence in American ideas and products that characterized the Federal era, along with the realization that building materials and needs were different in England and America, encouraged first Benjamin, and soon others, to produce their own native builders' guides. Benjamin's second and most famous book was proudly titled *The American Builder's Companion*.

In the preface to his *Practical Architecture*, published in 1833, Benjamin speaks plainly about his anticipated audience:

Those Carpenters in country villages who aspire to eminence in their business, having no Architect to consult, are under the necessity of studying the science thoroughly and without a master. To them, therefore, is this book peculiarly adapted; for it contains the prin-

ciples of many expensive folios, condensed into a narrow space and applied to modern practice.

Benjamin created a new and eminently usable kind of book by combining the wisdom of the high-style folios with the humbler, how-to advice of the builders' books. Judging by the number of details and even entire buildings traceable to his designs, Benjamin may be said to have achieved the goal he enunciated in *The Practical House Carpenter* of 1830. In its introduction he pledged to make "a practical treatise on that subject [architecture], adapted to the present style of building in our own country." His characterization of "carpenters in country villages who aspire to eminence in their business" is the perfect description of men like Lindsley and Carter in Morristown, and dozens of others throughout New Jersey who rose to local eminence with the help of Benjamin's new American books.

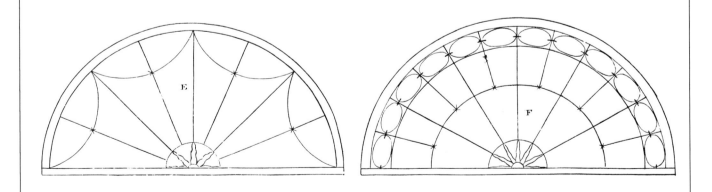

THE PATTERN BOOK COMES OF AGE

Andrew Jackson Downing, Tastemaker

On November 2, 1848, Stephen Youngs, whose acquaintance we have made already, inspected a house that he had no part in building. It belonged to his nephew, George Vail, who had built it on the willow-fringed shore of Speedwell Lake in Morristown, opposite his family's Speedwell Iron Works. Here is how George's house struck Stephen on that November afternoon: "We likewise went into George Vail's new house and viewed it throughout, a very roomy convenient house inside and a very odd formed house outside as all may see."[1]

In the spirit of an earlier day, the practical old carpenter-builder, who was just shy of his seventy-fourth birthday, praised roominess and convenience above all else. "Willow Hall" (Fig. 40), as George named his new country seat, is still impressive today,

Fig. 40. By building Willow Hall of a glacial conglomerate called puddingstone, George Vail added color and textural interest to the A. J. Downing design he copied.

although hardly eccentric in appearance to the modern eye. Built of purple puddingstone, a glacial conglomerate of local origin, the house is a rectangular block with deep, bracketed eaves, a large center gable, and paired windows. Its exterior is enlivened by a tented roof above the entry, bracketed window heads, tiny third-floor balconies, and semi-octagonal bays on the gable ends. These playful features might well seem "odd formed" to a man accustomed all his long life to the sober utility of houses like the Vail Homestead (Fig. 41), which still stands across the road from Willow Hall.

The features that seemed peculiar to Stephen Youngs were derived from neither of the architectural strains that had molded his entire building career—classical sources and the folk-building tradition. To design his house George Vail turned not to an architect or a local builder, not to the well-used volumes of Benjamin or Lafever that had been so successful in promoting the Federal and Greek Revival modes of neoclassicism, but to a new and revolutionary book written by a man who changed the way Americans thought about and built their houses. Willow Hall was taken directly from Design V, "A Cottage Villa in the Bracketed Mode," in *Cottage Residences*, written in 1842 by Andrew Jackson Downing (Fig. 42). Downing was the premier spokesman for a burgeoning Romantic taste in America. His book, especially in its dedication to the picturesque, was a cogent summary of the reaction against a century of Georgian, Federal, and Greek Revival neoclassicism. Full of house plans and elevations coupled with commentary on furniture styles, wall and window treatments, and landscaping,

Fig. 41. A simple wooden farmhouse, the Vail homestead was remodeled by Judge Stephen Vail, who added a Greek Revival portico to the entrance.

DESIGN V.

A COTTAGE VILLA IN THE BRACKETED MODE.

Fig. 36

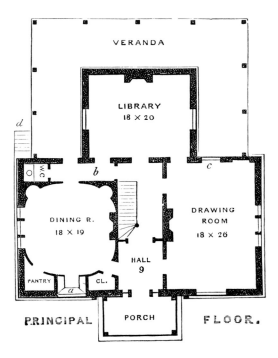

Fig. 42. Andrew Jackson Downing's attention to interiors is reflected in the oval dining room of this design for a cottage villa, one of many details George Vail copied faithfully when he built Willow Hall.

Cottage Residences was the first American pattern book to describe fully an ideal, middle-class suburban home.

Willow Hall was one of the first important New Jersey houses taken in its entirety from Downing's book. It did not stand alone for long. By the middle of the 1850s, choice villa lots throughout the state were sprouting houses in the fashionable new Romantic taste, influenced by Downing's third book, *The Architecture of Country Houses* (1850), and similar books by others. To understand Andrew Jackson Downing's influence and his role in vanquishing classicism, we can begin by examining a quartet of houses built within a decade and several miles of one another, each inconceivable without Downing's Romantic vision. They are Willow Hall, Acorn Hall, Wisteria Lodge and The Willows. Their appearance and how they came to be built tell volumes about the new Romantic age.

Willow Hall, the earliest of the four, was built in 1848. George Vail, its new owner, was the son of Stephen Vail, who had made his fame by manufacturing the engine for the *Savannah*, the first

Fig. 43. The large wooden brackets that lent Downing's "Bracketed Mode" its name are an essential feature of Willow Hall.

steamship to cross the Atlantic. In 1844 George became chief proprietor of the Speedwell Iron Works, a responsibility that did not
prevent him from pursuing a political career as well. After serving
in the New Jersey legislature, he was elected to two terms in the
United States House of Representatives, followed by an appoint-
ment as United States consul to Glasgow.[2] A forward-looking in-
dustrialist and an honored politician, George Vail also led the way
in architecture.

About Stephen Vail, George's father, it was said, "As an early
leader of industrial America, Stephen had acquired great wealth.
But the taste for luxury, leisure and extravagant display . . . never
touched his disciplined life."[3] Like his father, George used his
wealth with moderation. Although Willow Hall stood in stark stylistic contrast to the Vail family homestead, it embodied all the
attributes of good taste and dignity without ostentation inherent in
Downing's persuasive books. In fact, Downing might have been
describing George Vail and Willow Hall in 1850 when he wrote in
The Architecture of Country Houses: "But the true home still remains
to us . . . the beautiful, rural, unostentatious, moderate home of a
country gentleman, large enough to minister to all the wants, necessities and luxuries of a republican, and not too large or too luxu-
rious to warp the life and manners of his children."

Downing was indebted to the most important English theo-
rists of the day for his notion that Good Architecture produced a
Good Society, a philosophy that continued, under Downing's influence, to color the early Romantic Revival and its pattern-book ex-
ponents. Always the practical American, however, he refused to let
moral philosophy seduce him away from mundane requirements.
In *Cottage Residences*, Downing's description of the design that
George Vail chose for Willow Hall (Fig. 43) reveals his customary
interest in the way appearance is molded by environmental needs:

> The strongly marked character it has is derived mainly from
> the bold projection of the roof, supported by ornamental
> brackets, and from the employment of brackets in various
> other parts of the building. . . . The coolness and dryness of
> the upper story, afforded by the almost veranda-like roof, will
> render this a delightful feature in all parts of the country
> where the summers are hot, and the sun very bright during
> the long days of that season.

Named the "Bracketed mode" by Downing, this kind of
dwelling was based loosely on Italian models. It appealed to him
so strongly that he observed, in *Cottage Residences*, "Indeed, we
think a very ingenious architect might produce an *American cottage
style* by carefully studying the capabilities of this mode, so abounding in picturesqueness and so easily executed." In the village of

Fig. 44. Wisteria Lodge was one with its landscape. Downing's books insisted on this fusion of art and nature.

Madison, within an easy carriage ride of Willow Hall, stood another cottage villa "abounding in picturesqueness." Wisteria Lodge, demolished in 1991, was less indebted than Willow Hall to traditional Italian precedents; it more clearly exemplified the American cottage style that Downing prophesied. Its sheltering, bracketed cross-gables and long, wooden tent-roofed verandas supported on filigree cast-iron posts dripping with wisteria (Fig. 44) were the perfect realization of the bracketed mode allied to its natural setting.

Like George Vail, the builder of Wisteria Lodge was a man of consequence. Francis Stebbins Lathrop had made a fortune in the dry goods business, which he abandoned in 1853 to become president of the Union Mutual Fire and Marine Insurance Company of New York. Like other railroad commuters who worked in the city and lived in the country, Lathrop cultivated an interest in horticulture. His avocation eventually grew into a business, making him

Andrew Jackson Downing

Unlike Lafever and Benjamin, his two most important American predecessors, Andrew Jackson Downing (1815–1852) was not a builder-architect but a horticulturist and "landscape gardener," a calling that fashioned his belief in the inviolable unity of a dwelling and its setting. In modern terms, he would be a landscape architect. Downing's credo at its simplest is set forth in *Cottage Residences*, where he wrote: "I wish to inspire all persons with a love of beautiful forms, and a desire to assemble them around their daily walks of life. I wish them to appreciate how superior is the charm of that home where we discover the tasteful cottage or villa, and the well designed and neatly kept garden or grounds, full of beauty and harmony." Because he was not trained as a draftsman, Downing's first house designs were drawn by others to his specifications; later he published designs by such respected architects as John Notman, Richard Upjohn, Gervase Wheeler, Alexander Jackson Davis, and Calvert Vaux.

In his own person Downing was the quintessential Romantic figure, as this engraving by J. Halpin in the National Portrait Gallery suggests. His flowing hair and dark complexion inspired one contemporary to call his looks Spanish. His tragic drowning at the age of thirty-six while trying to rescue fellow passengers from a steamboat wreck on the Hudson River served only to enhance his reputation. During his brief career he was rewarded with ample success by an attentive public that took his role as tastemaker as seriously as Downing himself did. In 1850 he invited a young English architect, Calvert Vaux, to establish with him the firm of Vaux and Downing. At the time of his death he was preparing landscape plans for the Smithsonian Institution and the Mall at Washington, D.C., the two most prestigious commissions of the day.

The National Portrait Gallery, Smithsonian Institution

More significant, ultimately, than his nationally prominent work was Downing's fascination with the kind of modest dwelling that eventually grew into the American suburban ideal. He did not conceive of architecture in a vacuum, but visualized houses whose inhabitants would be encouraged to make the right decisions about the correct kind of life, a correlation between morality and art typical of the Romantic movement. This architectural and social "expressiveness" was the basis of his contribution to the pattern-book movement and illuminates the tangle of styles that sometimes seems to divide rather than unify American architecture of the Romantic age.

one of the first commercial rose growers in Madison, a town famed later in the nineteenth century as "The Rose City." In 1869 New Jersey governor Theodore Fitz Randolph named Lathrop an associate judge of the Court of Errors and Appeals. He served in the Court of Pardons until his death in 1882 at the age of seventy-six. He had earned such regard that his funeral prompted adjournment of the New Jersey legislature so that its members might pay their last respects.

In November of 1856 Judge Lathrop's only son, Frank, married Isabel Gibbons; the following year the judge had Wisteria Lodge built as their wedding gift. Isabel was accustomed to domestic grandeur. Her family home, probably the most splendid Greek Revival mansion in New Jersey, is now the administration building for Drew University. Whether her father-in-law's gift of a fashionable cottage-villa pleased her has gone unrecorded, but Judge Lathrop's interest in architecture seems to have been more than a passing fancy: as president of the Board of Managers for the State Asylum for the Insane, Lathrop supervised construction of the massive new asylum in Morris Plains, begun in 1874. Its designer, the Philadelphia architect and pattern-book author Samuel Sloan, became a friend, and served as a pallbearer at Lathrop's funeral.[4] Despite this intriguing connection with Sloan and the strong Downingesque character of the house, no direct pattern-book match or architect's commission has been discovered for Wisteria Lodge. These circumstances make the estate's tenant cottage (Fig. 45) all the more curious. It was almost a line-for-line copy of Design II, "Small Bracketed Cottage" (Fig. 46), with some features borrowed from Design I, "A Laborer's Cottage," in Downing's *The Architecture of Country Houses*, proof that Judge Lathrop was conversant with the latest in pattern-book taste.

The names "Willow" and "Wisteria" remind us that Downing's horticultural training encouraged him to promote the organic unity of a house and its setting. This principle is apparent from the landscape elements in Downing's illustrations, which make them so different from those of Benjamin and Lafever, whose houses were set forth in plates with no suggestion of natural features. Acorn Hall (Fig. 47), the third house in our quartet, was named to celebrate its picturesque location, framed by giant black oaks and copper beeches, above the Whippany River. Downing prescribed just such a setting in *Cottage Residences*, where he remarked that "the beautiful wooded situations on the banks of our fine rivers are, many of them, admirably suited to an Italian villa of this kind." Built in 1853 for Louise and John Schermerhorn on what were then the outskirts of Morristown, Acorn Hall began as a small, three-bay house. In 1860 it was remodeled by its second owners, Augustus and Mary Bolles Crane.[5] Like Willow Hall and Wisteria Lodge, brackets figured prominently in the design of Acorn Hall, but

Modest Cottages

Pattern-book houses like this tiny board-and-batten laborer's cottage in Rocky Hill (*below left*), which resembles Designs I and II from Downing's *The Architecture of Country Houses* (see Fig. 46), are often overlooked by architectural historians because of their extreme simplicity. It is these simplest examples, too, that often have been altered beyond recognition.

Rarely does one find a standing example of a house like Downing's "Suburban Cottage" from *Cottage Residences* (*right*). Although now unrecognizable, a house built from this design still stands in the Methodist Camp Meeting community of Mount Tabor, identifiable today only by comparison with an 1880s illustration owned by the Mount Tabor Historical Society (*below right*).

The owner of the cottage was S. M. Long, secretary of the board of trustees and president of the Mount Tabor Social Union. The reason that a prominent gentleman built such a modest dwelling is explained by the fact that this was merely Mr. Long's summer cottage, quite roomy by Mount Tabor standards, where many building lots were no more than twenty-five feet wide. The construction date, 1882, may seem late for a house copied from an 1842 pattern book, but a new edition of *Cottage Residences* was brought out in 1873, a continuing testimony to A. J. Downing's appeal to the American home builder.

DESIGN I.

A SUBURBAN COTTAGE.

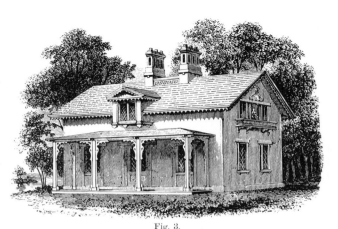

Fig. 3.

Downing would have described it not as a house in the bracketed mode but, specifically, as "A Villa in the Italian Style, Bracketed," the title of Design VI in his *Cottage Residences* (Fig. 48), the plate that influenced the remodeled Acorn Hall. The towered Italianate villa, introduced to American architecture for the first time in that illustration, became one of the most emulated house types of the 1850s and 1860s. According to architectural historian Jane B. Davies, "This very influential design for a villa in the avant-garde Italianate style featured three important innovations: a new, irregular house shape, board-and-batten siding, and brackets . . . the house shape was Downing's concept, a new pattern in America: a deliberately L-shaped house, with the angle toward the front, and moreover, a tower in the angle."[6]

Although Acorn Hall could not have existed without Downing's design, its appearance is typical of how pattern-book models were simplified by tradition-minded builders. In this case, a talented local carpenter, Ashbel Bruen, freely interpreted the architectural fashion of the day for the Cranes, dispensing with board-and-batten siding in favor of clapboard but relying heavily on brackets (Fig. 49) and details like the tented balcony roof to express the chosen Italianate flavor. Two interpolations seem all Bruen's own: an octagonal rather than a square tower, and bold, wooden arabesques, almost a folk version of high-style cast iron porch ornament. Significant, too, is the placement of the tower. Centered on the facade rather than placed in the angle of an L-plan, it resulted from Bruen's efforts to modernize the 1853 Schermerhorn house.

The most spectacular of these four early villas was The Willows, built in 1853 in Morris Township, on the road to Mendham. If George Vail's house had impressed some as "odd formed," The Willows must have set the neighborhood agog (Fig. 50). Neither Bracketed nor Italianate, it illustrated the third major architectural mode favored by the pattern-book authors of the 1850s, Gothic Revival. Vail, Lathrop, and Crane were forward-looking but essentially conservative entrepreneurs. Col. Joseph Warren Revere (Fig. 51) was a different order of man entirely. Grandson of the patriot Paul Revere, he was an artist, adventurer, soldier, and soldier of fortune, whose military career ended in a Civil War court-martial. Revere's choice of an exceptionally individualistic pattern-book design reflected the picaresque character he presented in his autobiography, *Keel and Saddle*—a figure who might have modeled for what Downing called in *Country Houses* "men of imagination—men whose aspirations never leave them at rest—men whose ambition and energy will give them no peace within the bounds of mere rationality. These are the men for picturesque villas—country houses with high roofs, steep gables, unsymmetrical and capricious forms." Downing's "high roofs and steep gables" sounds like a press agent's description of The Willows. Revere must have

Fig. 45. Judge Francis Lathrop's tenant cottage for Wisteria Lodge incorporated the board-and-batten siding found in Downing's designs but absent from most New Jersey houses.

derived great satisfaction from thinking of himself as Downing's "really original man living in an original and characteristic house."

Even though it suggests his architectural precepts, The Willows is not based on a design published by Downing himself. Instead, Revere turned to a book titled *Rural Homes*, written in 1851 by Gervase Wheeler.[7] Revere adopted Wheeler's pattern-book design (Fig. 52) almost line for line, but added a service wing that made the house even more picturesquely "unsymmetrical" than its author had intended. Ashbel Bruen, the talented carpenter-builder who would later remodel Acorn Hall, transformed Wheeler's pattern-book illustration to three-dimensional form, but it was Revere who made The Willows his personal creation in precisely

DESIGN II
SMALL BRACKETED COTTAGE

Fig. 9

PRINCIPAL FLOOR
Fig. 10.

Fig. 46. The L-shaped plan and projecting eaves of this tiny house impart a sense of style, but, as Downing maintained, it is the embowering vines that contribute a "home-like, domestic expression."

Fig. 47. Acorn Hall assumed the aspect of a towered Italianate villa when it was enlarged by Augustus and Mary Crane in 1860.

DESIGN VI.

A VILLA IN THE ITALIAN STYLE, BRACKETED.

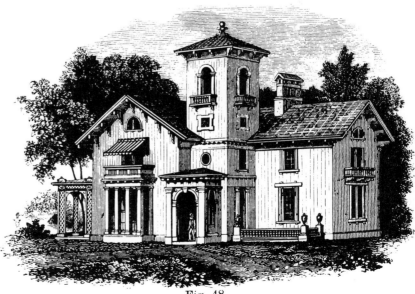

Fig. 48. The campanile, or tower, was an essential feature of Downing's "Villa in the Italian Style, Bracketed." The more common square tower pictured here inspired the octagonal variant added to Acorn Hall.

Fig. 48.

66

Fig. 49. One of the hallmarks of the Italianate style that Downing popularized was the bracket, shown here as bold ornamentation for Acorn Hall's tower.

the manner that Downing and his contemporaries encouraged. He painted the dining room himself with extraordinary trompe l'oeil murals depicting foodstuffs and game trophies; the front hall he painted (or had painted) with *faux boiserie*; he ordered the Revere family crest carved into the marble of the parlor fireplace; he paved the front hall with Minton encaustic tile (an early domestic use of that material in America), and for the same room he hired a wood-carver to execute a fantastical Gothic-style mantel and matching suite of furniture. Throughout the house he had doors and wood-work grained to simulate more expensive woods, some with burled effects.

Like Downing, Gervase Wheeler was interested in structure and building technology as well as style. Although Gothic Revival

Fig. 50. A two-storied traceried porch shades the front rooms of The Willows and establishes its Gothic identity.

to our eyes, The Willows was a thoroughly modern house for its time. In *Rural Homes*, Wheeler noted that the design was Gothic only insofar as its nominally historical motifs (principally its colossal porch tracery) "determine any distinctive style." He also made the very modern point that its construction was rational—that its major decorative elements arise from structural necessity: "The sharp gable over the side is framed so that the construction shows externally—this being no sham, but the actual framing of the roof within, the chamber ceilings of that part of the house being lathed upon the curved beams that support the roof."

Fig. 51. Col. Joseph Warren Revere expressed his own fierce individuality by choosing one of the era's most unusual pattern-book designs for his new house on the outskirts of Morristown. (Morris County Park Commission, Fosterfields Living Historical Farm)

Fig. 52. Embowered in trees, Gervase Wheeler's design displays a roof steeper than the one that Joseph Warren Revere built from it.

The Italianate Style

The existence of four remarkable houses within a carriage drive of one another, all built within the span of a decade, gave some notion of how quickly the new gospel of Romanticism had captured the imagination of New Jersey builders. Andrew Jackson Downing may have been the most influential of the early proponents of the picturesque, but he soon stood in the company of a host of colleagues and competitors. *Godey's Magazine* (later *Godey's Lady's Book*), perhaps the most widely read monthly magazine in America between 1840 and 1860, boasted in 1849 that "hundreds of cottages have been built from plans that we have published." In 1852, an author named Lewis F. Allen took up Downing's enthusiasm for the Italianate in a book called *Rural Architecture*. Allen claimed, "The Italian style of architecture, modified somewhat in pretension and extent, is admirably adapted to most parts of the United States. Its general lightness, openness, and freedom gives a wide range of choice; and its wings, verandas, and terraces, stretching off in any and almost every direction desired from the main building make it exceedingly appropriate for general use."

New Jersey owes its legacy of Italianate architecture to several sources. Two of the finest examples, "Prospect" and "Guernsey Hall," both in Princeton, are the work of John Notman, whose designs Downing published. Notman also enjoys the distinction of having designed the first important Italianate house in the United

States, a villa for Bishop George Washington Doane, built in Burlington in 1839. Other Italianate villas, built without direct involvement of an architect, were copied or adapted from the designs of the Philadelphia architect and pattern-book author Samuel Sloan. Like most of his contemporaries, Sloan published domestic designs in several Romantic styles, but his powerful Italianate designs were particularly influential in New Jersey. His book *The Model Architect* appeared first as a series of individual folios, published by E. S. Jones and Company of Philadelphia, beginning in 1851. Larger than most pattern books of the day and rich in drawings of

Fig. 53. Samuel Sloan designed this small Italianate villa with a centered tower recessed behind a pair of gabled pavilions.

details, *The Model Architect* was taken up avidly by a public eager for novelty, "good taste," and sound architectural advice, all of which Sloan furnished peerlessly.

In his essay "Italian Architecture," he described its pertinent features, noting that "throughout there is a tendency rather to boldness than minute decoration," an apt characterization of his own work. Two houses built in Plainfield illustrate the creative liberties that local builders took when adapting designs like Sloan's to the needs of their clients. The first, and more unusual, design was for a small villa that appeared as Design I in the first volume of *The Model Architect*. Its distinguishing feature is a tower (or "campanile," in Sloan's words) centered behind a pair of gabled, projecting blocks (Fig. 53). In his translation of Sloan's design, the Plainfield builder increased the shallow, Italianate roof pitch, a change that enabled him to gain an attic story while shedding the snow of New Jersey winters. For some less apparent reason he connected the two front-facing blocks so that the tower became less dominant (Fig. 54). Minor adjustments in fenestration and porch design are

Fig. 54. The details of this house in North Plainfield probably resembled Sloan's design more closely before alterations took place in the twentieth century. The porch, especially, has been changed.

typical of how carpenters simplified their pattern-book sources. Although the center tower with flanking pavilions is an uncommon design in pattern-book literature, it was not unique to Samuel Sloan. Downing had published a similar house by John Notman as Design IX in *Cottage Residences*, and John Riddell's "Villa No. 8" in his 1861 book, *Architectural Designs for Model Country Residences*, was another version. The similarity seems more than coincidental, for Notman, Sloan, and Riddell were all Philadelphians and must have been familiar with one another's work.

Scattered among several Plainfield neighborhoods are variations on two designs for stuccoed and towered Italianate villas. One

Design VI.   *Pl. XXI.*

Sam.l Sloan, Arch.t   P.S.Duval's Steam lith Press. Philad.a

PERSPECTIVE VIEW.

Fig. 55. In his design for a large villa Samuel Sloan made use of round-arched windows enriched with heavy moldings. The tower balcony is graced with the same kind of wooden awning roof found on the tower of Acorn Hall.

Fig. 56. Plainfield and North Plainfield abound with towered and stuccoed houses that resemble Sloan's designs. (John Grady)

was published by Sloan as Design VI in the first volume of *The Model Architect* (Fig. 55); the other is Riddell's "Villa No. 6." A house in the Crescent Avenue Historic District is an amplification rather than a reduction of Sloan's prototype. Here the builder increased the height by a full story, in the process changing the roof from hipped to gabled. In the built example, the tower arcade is composed of five instead of three windows, but the tented roof above the balcony is true to Sloan's design. More important than these adjustments, the Plainfield builder recognized and retained Sloan's basic compositional principles: the long horizontal porch, which anchors the house to the ground visually, and the centered tower, which contributes an essential, vertical thrust (Fig. 56).

The towered villa was the basis for the most picturesque Italianate compositions, but equally popular in some parts of New Jersey was the more classically disposed cubical villa, or "Italianate cube." Sloan's influence was felt here, too. His Design XLIV for a "Southern Mansion" from Volume II of *The Model Architect* was depicted amidst swaying palm trees (Fig. 57). Shorn of the finial atop the belvedere (Italian for "beautiful view"), it becomes

Fig. 57. Samuel Sloan decorated the four-square simplicity of his cubical Italianate "southern mansion" with curvilinear ornament on belvedere, eaves, window heads, and porch posts. New Jersey builders usually dispensed with such rococo filigree when they adapted Sloan's designs.

Fig. 58. The house built for George Allen in Cape May is one of New Jersey's finest cubical Italianate villas. It shares features in common with designs by both Sloan and Riddell.

FRONT ELEVATION

Fig. 59. Sloan's fellow Philadelphian John Riddell presented another version of the cubical Italianate house in his Architectural Designs *of 1861. Riddell emphasized the attic story with a row of paired and round-arched windows. (Athenaeum of Philadelphia)*

one possible model for the commanding house (Fig. 58) that contractor Henry Phillippi built for the Philadelphia dry-goods merchant George Allen in Cape May in the winter of 1863–64.[8] Although Sloan's design might have inspired the huge paired brackets and the full-length veranda, a plate from Riddell's book (Fig. 59) illustrates round-arched attic windows and a triple-arched belvedere exactly like George Allen's. Because of the resort's proximity to Philadelphia, most of its notable architecture was designed by architects from that city or builders who were influenced by the latest Philadelphia houses. In light of this well-known connection, it seems likely that Allen or Phillippi might have owned a copy of either Sloan's book or Riddell's, or both.

The adoption of designs disseminated through pattern books was not the province of successful merchants alone. Prosperous

Fig. 60. In The Model Architect *Samuel Sloan observed that a wide-spreading roof results in a fine architectural effect by its strong contrasts of light and shade. The cornice of the Holmes-Tallman house produces just such an effect.*

farmers were building pattern-book houses, too. The money that built the Holmes-Tallman House (Fig. 60) in Monroe Township in about 1860 came from agriculture instead of dry goods, but the same published sources that inspired George Allen's house must have guided the creation of its five-foot-high brackets and tall French windows leading to an airy veranda. Its belvedere was perfect for contemplating not palm trees but the endless central New Jersey fields that had produced the wealth that built it, a fine example of Romanticism melded with practicality.

Not every farmer could afford Italianate ostentation of the Holmes-Tallman kind, but the cubical house proved to be appealing in agricultural settings nonetheless. A much simpler version was popularized by a periodical called the *American Agriculturalist*, edited by the same Lewis Allen who had recommended the Italian-ate style "modified somewhat in pretension and extent." One of seventy agricultural magazines and newspapers in circulation before 1850, it appealed to forward-looking farmers striving to adopt scientific methods.[9] As part of an improved and rational rural order, architecture, too, became a topic of more than passing interest among such men. How many Jerseymen were subscribers in the 1850s and 1860s cannot be determined, but the simplified Italian-ate cube based on the *Agriculturalist's* 1859 "Dwelling house in the Italian Order" (Fig. 61) was-built again and again as the up-to-date ornament of many farms. Two nearly identical examples are found in Rocky Hill (Figs. 62 and 63), and a third stands nearby in Griggstown. The farming centers of Hightstown, Freehold, and Allentown are home to half a dozen slightly fancier town versions.

Some of the more grandiose designs published by Samuel Sloan, Calvert Vaux, and others reflected the beau ideal of Italian-ate architecture. Such designs, intended for masonry construction and many servants, were not often built, at least in New Jersey, where the secret of the Italianate style's success was precisely the adaptability that Lewis Allen claimed for it. Cottage-villas rather than mansions were the mainstay of the Italianate in most places, where houses of middling size and pretension appealed strongly to both suburbanites and more rural home builders. In the farm country in and around Rocky Hill are two houses in the "Anglo Norman Style" (Figs. 64 and 65), clearly a variant of the Italianate. Both were modeled on the same pattern-book design, Plate XXXVIII in Volume II of William H. Ranlett's *The Architect* (Fig. 66).

The better documented of the two houses (Fig. 64) was built between 1860 and 1862 by Peter L. Van Derveer, whose grandfather had begun buying land in the Millstone Valley in 1760, and eventually amassed four hundred acres.[10] The valley was still steeped in Dutch traditions and folkways in the eighteenth century, but by the opening of the nineteenth century most Dutch farmers were indistinguishable, except for their surnames and surviving old-style barns, from their "English" neighbors. Not only had New Jersey's prosperous farmers abandoned ethnic connections by this date, they had begun to lay aside traditional architecture as well, a tendency illustrated by Peter Van Derveer's adoption of a high-style pattern-book design. Although not ostentatious, Van Derveer's house was fitted out with blue and red etched glass, Minton tiles, marble mantels, and elaborate plaster ceiling medallions—decorations of greater elegance than even his successful father could have imagined. These manufactured wares were an indication of how far the industrialization of American architecture and household decor had come by the 1860s. The accelerating pattern of production and consumption was capitalized on by pattern books, which described in detail the array of mass-produced goods

Fig. 61. (right) *Still recognizable as a cubical Italianate house, this stripped-down version was published in the* American Agriculturalist *as a dwelling suitable for a practical farmer.*

Figs. 62 (opposite) *and 63* (above). *Based on the design in the* American Agriculturalist, *these two farmhouses in Rocky Hill show just how much simpler than the imposing Sloan and Riddell versions the Italiante cube might become.*

that could be combined to create the genteel and fashionable domestic environment.

Though its designer described it as "Anglo Norman," the house that Van Derveer built was yet another variation on A. J. Downing's towered Italianate villa. Although it would finally lose its cachet during the last quarter of the nineteenth century, the persistence of that versatile Italianate archetype was still evident in 1876, when Daniel Topping Atwood's third book, *Modern American Homesteads*, was published. Atwood's Plate 11 is a delightfully

Figs. 64 (above) *and 65* (top, opposite). *A particular pattern-book design often caught the fancy of builders within hailing distance of one another. Identical but for insignificant details, one of these villas was built on the main street in the village of Rocky Hill, the other as a fashionable farmhouse a few miles away.*

idiosyncratic version of the towered villa (Fig. 67). Its blocky massing and robust details, most of them explicitly neoclassical, impart something of the solidity of masonry to this frame house. Especially appealing is the mirror-image detailing of the tower, with arches both above and *below* the windows, an eccentric Atwood trademark. One of a number of Atwood designs built in Tenafly, it became the home of Dr. J. J. Haring (Fig. 68) and stood through the first half of the twentieth century.

Fig. 66. The towered Italiante villa inspired variations like this "Anglo Norman" house. Both New Jersey builders who constructed houses from the same William Ranlett design duplicated the emphatic chevron motif beneath the eaves, clearly delineated in the pattern-book drawings.

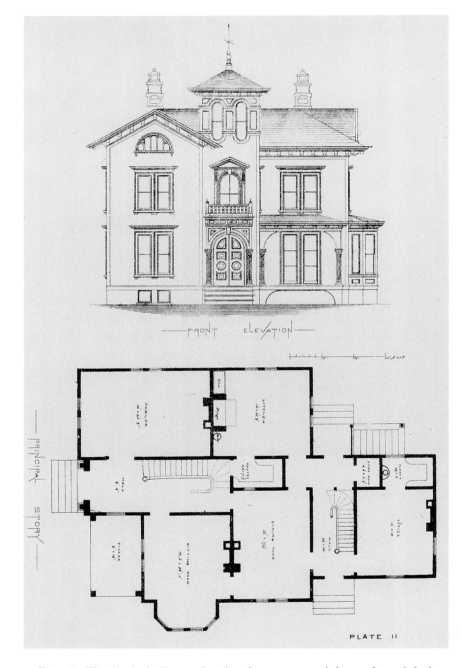

Fig. 67. The classical pilasters framing the entrance and the porch, and the large attic lunette (a Diocletian window) suggest that Daniel T. Atwood was familiar with the ancient Roman sources of the Italianate style. (Avery Architectural and Fine Arts Library, Columbia University in the City of New York)

Fig. 68. The children gathered in front of Dr. J. J. Haring's house are not his progeny: the house later became a school run by his daughter. (Reprinted with permission from the Borough of Tenafly, Tenafly Public Library Collection)

Paradoxically, the towered Italianate villa became even more popular when shorn of its tower, for Downing's "invention" of the L-shaped plan proved to be one of his most enduring legacies. Without towers, L-plan houses appeared in almost every pattern book published between the 1850s and the 1870s, and were built again and again in New Jersey towns. In many cases, these houses remained recognizably Italianate by virtue of brackets and other details; in other cases their Italianate heritage had virtually disappeared. Design 1 (Fig. 69) in *Woodward's National Architect* is typical of many. With some adjustments, it might have been the model for an exceptionally well-preserved example in Plainfield (Fig. 70).

Fig. 69. By the end of the 1860s many nominally Italianate designs had lost the blocky solidity favored by Downing and Sloan. The very flat brackets and very thin porch posts of this L-plan cottage from Woodward's National Architect *presage the angularity of the Stick Style.*

Design No. 1.   Plate No. 1.

Fig. 70. Typical of an entire class of L-plan houses that retained some vestiges of their Italianate ancestry is this Plainfield example; it shares many features with the design from Woodward's National Architect.

The Gothic Revival and Its Offspring

Isolated Gothic references were found in American eighteenth-century architecture before the advent of anything like a full-blown Gothic Revival and long before a hint of the Italianate style. In the nineteenth century, however, pattern books coupled the Gothic and Italianate: "The Rural Gothic style, characterized mainly by pointed gables, and the Italian, by projecting roofs, balconies, and terraces, are much the most beautiful modes for our country residences," reflected Andrew Jackson Downing in *Cottage Residences*. Downing published designs for both styles and, in the best Romantic tradition, ascribed different associative qualities to each. About the Gothic he observed:

> Not a little of the delight of beautiful buildings to a cultivated mind grows out of the *sentiment* of architecture, or the associations connected with certain styles. Thus the sight of an old English villa will call up in the mind of one familiar with the history of architecture, the times of the Tudors, or of "Merry England," in the days of Elizabeth. The mingled quaintness, beauty, and picturesqueness of the exterior, no less than the oaken wainscot, curiously carved furniture, and fixtures of the interior of such a dwelling, when harmoniously complete, seem to transport one back to a past age . . . in which the shadowy lines of poetry and reality seem strangely interwoven and blended.[11]

Of the two styles, Gothic and Italian, the Gothic Revival was the more "literary." Its most ambitious exemplars (the apogee of the style is A. J. Davis's "Lyndhurst," on the Hudson River in Tarrytown, New York) are linked to the historical visions of writers like Sir Walter Scott and the narrative force of Hudson River School painters like Thomas Cole and New Jersey's Asher B. Durand. To make its maximum impact, the high-style Gothic dwelling required expansive size, masonry construction, and a proliferation of crockets, carvings, pointed windows, and upthrusting pinnacles, features beyond the means of the ordinary successful professional or merchant contemplating construction of a villa. Out of the desire for the concentrated picturesqueness of the Gothic without its burdensome expense grew the Gothic Revival cottage. As early as his 1837 book, *Rural Residences*, A. J. Davis was experimenting with designs for modest Gothic cottages, and four years later Downing published several of Davis's Gothic designs in *A Treatise on the Theory and Practice of Landscape Gardening*. The following year, with the appearance of *Cottage Residences*, the distillation of the Davis and Downing cottage collaboration began to reach an enormous public. Two of the designs in *Cottage Residences* which became prototypes for countless small Gothic houses are Design II, "A Cottage in the English or Rural Gothic Style" (Fig. 71), and the similar but simpler Design IV, "An Ornamental Farm House."

The Gothic identity of both designs is concentrated on a steeply pitched gable centered on the facade. With this single image standing in for the entire array of Gothic ornament and form,

DESIGN II.

A COTTAGE IN THE ENGLISH OR RURAL GOTHIC STYLE.

Fig. 9.

Fig. 71. A. J. Downing neatly summed up his admiration for the rural Gothic style by describing Design II from Cottage Residences *in these words: "The elevation of this cottage is in the English cottage style, so generally admired for the picturesqueness evinced in its tall gables ornamented by handsome verge-boards and finials, its neat or fanciful chimney tops, its latticed windows, and other striking features, showing how the genius of pointed or Gothic architecture may be chastened or moulded into forms for domestic habitation."*

Fig. 72. A Gothic cottage designed by A. J. Davis for Llewellyn Park later became the boyhood home of another great American architect, Charles McKim. His Quaker mother had this to say about Davis's design: "The house is rather fanciful for my taste; it was built for an artist; it has a funny pitched roof and clustered chimneys and bull's-eye windows, and niches for statuettes, and all sorts of artistic arrangements that don't quite suit my plain taste."

builders might add decorative elaboration (intricate bargeboards, pointed windows) as their budgets permitted. The clearest New Jersey statement of the Gothic cottage archetype is a house designed in 1859 by Davis himself for a landscape painter named Edward W. Nichols (Fig. 72). It is the offspring of the earlier Davis-Downing designs in *Cottage Residences*. The site Nichols chose for his cottage was in a brand-new community called Llewellyn Park, in West Orange, where Davis designed several houses. The brainchild of Llewellyn Haskell, a wealthy importer with a taste for the Romantic, Llewellyn Park was the first planned residential community of note in the United States based on the very principles of picturesque architecture and landscape that Davis and

Downing had hoped would become commonplace. At first one of only a handful of villas and cottages set amidst eight hundred acres of forest, ravines, and rambles, Nichols's house was the ideal realization of what Haskell called "country houses for city people." The property owners, fashioned "proprietors"—men of "taste and wealth," according to Haskell—were mostly railroad commuters who sought refuge from their urban, workaday surroundings in a parklike environment filled with suitably picturesque dwellings.

Once we recognize the steeply pitched gable as the hallmark of the Gothic cottage style, it is easy to see how much of New Jersey's pattern-book architecture was animated by that single element. Although pattern-book authors presented designs for new houses, they realized that old houses might be made new as well. One of the most significant Gothic Revival transformations of an earlier house is The Hermitage, in Ho-Ho-Kus (Fig. 73). Dr. Elijah

Fig. 73. Elijah Rosencrantz's eighteenth-century family home was built of brownstone, a material that suited perfectly William Ranlett's Gothic renovations.

Fig. 74. The gently rambling mass of Ranlett's design for The Hermitage seems everywhere punctuated by gables.

Fig. 75. Ranlett's engraving of The Hermitage depicts the "rich gables breaking out from among the intricacy of tall stems and shadowy foliage," which A. J. Downing had described so persuasively in a similar context.

Rosencrantz, Jr., entrusted the transformation of his eighteenth-century family home to the New York architect, William Ranlett. Its red sandstone masonry construction, typical of Dutch houses in Bergen County, was a fortunate circumstance, since few cottage builders enjoyed the ability to design with stone, a material praised by Downing and Davis, especially for the Gothic Revival style.

To raise the horizontal mass of the existing house toward some semblance of Gothic verticality, Ranlett relied on multiple gables (Fig. 74) Elaborated .with bargeboards and aspiring finials, these gables became the chief feature of Dr. Rosencrantz's cottage, an apt illustration for Downing's observation in *Cottage Residences* that "Whoever has seen one of these cottages [in the old English style], with its rich gables breaking out from among the intricacy of tall

Fig. 76. George E. Woodward's Hull-Brown cottage blends with its surroundings in the best tradition of Romantic landscape design.

DESIGN No. 1.

FIG. 1.—*Front Elevation.*

FIG. 2.—*End Elevation.*

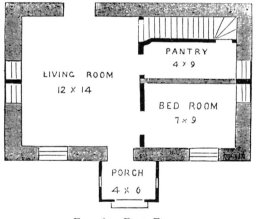

FIG. 3.—*First Floor.*

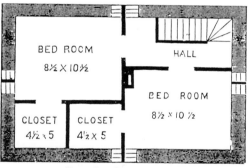

FIG. 4.—*Second Floor.*

Fig. 77. The roof of Woodward's cottage design is finished with clipped ends, sometimes called "jerkinhead" gables.

stems and shadowy foliage, will readily confess that he has rarely beheld anything more harmonious and delightful than the charming effect thereby produced." When Ranlett completed the enlargement and modernization in 1848 he was sufficiently pleased with the result to publish it, one of a number of designs he issued serially and finally collected as a book, *The Architect*, in 1851 (Fig. 75). This exposure made Dr. Rosencrantz's newly fashionable house a model for other builders and clients.[12]

Another gabled cottage (Fig. 76), also built of stone, which looks as if it might have been remodeled from a tiny, earlier house, was in fact built from scratch about 1867 in Tenafly, where several pattern-book authors were hard at work. Its designer was George E. Woodward, who published it as Design No. 1 in his 1865 book, *Woodward's Country Homes* (Fig. 77). Although rather earthbound in appearance for the Gothic style, this small house (probably a dependency on the Hull-Brown estate) exudes the air of quaintness the nineteenth century so admired in cottage dwellings.

Built a few years later in the same town from a design by

Fig. 78. Daniel T. Atwood's own house proved an effective billboard for his talents: a dozen more Atwood houses were built in Tenafly soon afterward.

Fig. 79. Atwood's steep gables imply a me-dieval-inspired, almost fairy-tale direct-ness, a quality emphasized by the naive character of the wood engraving. (Avery Ar-chitectural and Fine Arts Library, Colum-bia University in the City of New York)

Daniel Topping Atwood, another locally active pattern-book au-thor, was a house for an owner who could never get enough gables (Fig. 78). The design appeared in *Atwood's Country and Suburban Houses*, which was published in 1871, just two years before the final edition of Downing's ever-popular *Cottage Residences*. Like many of the gables depicted by Downing, Atwood's roofs for this design are high, steep, and unmistakably Gothic, and he makes them the principal motif of the entire house. Composed of two massive cross-gables on a T-shaped plan, with two additional wall-dormer gables lighting the main bedrooms, the house is far more verti-cal than Woodward's stumpy Hull-Brown cottage. Atwood's triple-gabled facade (Fig. 79) is a motif that recurs throughout the later history of New Jersey's pattern-book houses.

The gables and other features of the Gothic Revival were not to everyone's liking. Lewis F. Allen, an apologist for the Italianate, refused to countenance the coexistence of both styles. In *Rural Architecture*, his practical book for practical farmers, he fulminated against the Gothic:

Many of the designs recently introduced for the imitation of builders are full of angles and all sorts of zig-zag lines, which although they may add to the variety of style, or relieve the monotony of straight and continuous lines, are carried to a needless excess, expensive in their construction, and entail infinite trouble upon the owner or occupant, in the repairs they subject him to, in the leakage continually occurring, against which last, either of wind or rain, it is almost impossible to guard. And what, let us ask, are the benefits of a parcel of needless gables and peaked windows, running up like owl's ears, above the eaves of a house, except to create expense, and invite leakage and decay.[13]

Allen did have a point. Complex (Gothic, let us say) roofs do have a tendency to leak more than simple (Italianate, for example) roofs. Was there a way to be recognizably Gothic while satisfying Allen's practical requirements? One cottage variant that incorporates both style and utility is a house type that, like the Davis-

Design XII. *Pl. LIII.*

DESIGN FOR A COTTAGE.

Sam.¹ Sloan Arch.ᵗ   P S Duval's Steam lith press Ph.

Fig. 80. Samuel Sloan's versatility is demonstrated by his design for a small Gothic cottage, dissimilar in every way from the large Italianate houses for which he is better known.

Downing prototype represented by the Nichols house in Llewellyn Park, makes the center gable emblematic of the style. Sometimes it has a projecting center pavilion or bay, sometimes not. One of the finest surviving examples of this type stands in Shrewsbury. Copied with unusual fidelity from Design XII in volume 1 of Samuel Sloan's *The Model Architect*, it gains an extra sense of verticality from its board-and-batten siding, a popular pattern-book material rarely used in New Jersey (Fig. 80). Both Sloan and his faithful Shrewsbury copier enlivened even the board-and-batten cladding with Gothic arches above the ground-floor windows and below the center gable. The addition of louvered blinds is typical of how a tradition-minded builder might vernacularize and practicalize a published house design (Fig. 81).

Another Gothic design that avoids the excesses Allen complained of is Downing's "Symmetrical Cottage," published as

Fig. 81. Apart from the addition of louvered blinds, the New Jersey builder of this Shrewsbury house translated Sloan's pattern-book design with rare exactitude. It was built about 1860 for Dr. Peter Campbell.

DESIGN VII
SYMMETRICAL COTTAGE

Fig. 27

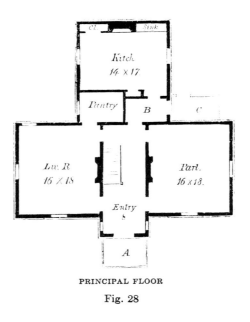

PRINCIPAL FLOOR

Fig. 28

Fig. 82. Although rambling asymmetry was a Romantic architectural ideal, A. J. Downing in his designs for small cottages concentrated picturesque details within a traditional, symmetrical frame.

Design VII in *The Architecture of Country Houses* (Fig. 82). Although the house is dressed with quatrefoil bargeboards and diamond-paned windows, its roof is mostly free of "angles and zig-zags." Its picturesque charms prompted the elders of the Colt's Neck Reformed Church to adopt it for their parsonage in 1857. Their carpenter executed a version faithful to Downing's design in all important particulars (Fig. 83).

Despite houses like these, the later history of Gothic Revival domestic architecture in New Jersey is one of even greater simplification. As Gothic decorative elements grew increasingly spare, they were assimilated into the genericized mainstream of pattern-book styles, becoming less and less "historic." In the process, Gothic lost most of its associations with chivalry, Christian virtue, and medieval romance, becoming a decorative appliqué instead of the architectural moral imperative its early apologists had had in mind. Take, for example, the Morristown home of Christopher Raymond Perry Rodgers (Fig. 84), commander-in-chief of the Pacific Squadron and the nephew of commodores John Rodgers and

Fig. 83. In 1857 the Colt's Neck Reformed Church commissioned carpenter Austin Patterson to build a parsonage. Church and builder agreed on a design from Downing's The Architecture of Country Houses.

Oliver H. and Matthew C. Perry. Built about 1852, Rodgers's house, especially its center gable dressed with fancy bargeboards, may trace its design to several of the simpler "Rural Gothic" cottages published by Downing. Its gable, however, is not really steep enough to be typically Gothic, while its circular and round-arched windows and striped porch roof are more typically Italianate.

As early as the 1860s, this kind of Gothic-Italianate hybrid was becoming a common and affordable alternative to the more historically correct versions of either style. A plate, originally printed in color, from John Riddell's 1861 book, *Architectural Designs*, depicts a house with a Gothic gable and an Italianate striped roof like the one that Rodgers had built (Fig. 85). The jigsawn bargeboard common to both Rodgers's house and Riddell's design may be the clue to their popularity. As the emergence of steam-powered woodworking tools made architectural enrichment cheaper and easier to acquire, middle-class home builders grew to prize abundant ornament more than style per se. With the help of industrialized architectural machinery like jigsaws, planers, and routers, Gothic Revival gave way to a promiscuously ornamented "Carpenter's Gothic." As a result, an entire class of center-gabled and bracketed Gothic-Italianate cottages and farmhouses became typical of the New Jersey landscape.

Fig. 84. Commodore and Mrs. Christopher Raymond Perry Rodgers take their ease on a verandah fringed with wooden tassels and supported by latticed posts entwined with fragrant creepers. (Ann and James Yardley)

Fig. 85. John Riddell presented even modest cottage designs like this with masonry walls, an ideal usually ignored by New Jersey builders, as proven by the clapboard walls of the Christopher Raymond Perry Rodgers house. (The Athenaeum of Philadelphia)

Such houses bore only tenuous connections to historical precedent but enjoyed the great virtue of affordability, especially important in New Jersey, with its growing market for suburban housing. Although they boasted of their egalitarian goals, the authors of the Golden Age of the pattern book—Downing, Sloan, Wheeler, Ranlett and others—appealed most readily to an affluent audience made up of men like George Vail, Joseph Warren Revere, and Elijah Rosencrantz instead of the average householder. Only with the emergence of new building technologies, which made new styles possible, did architectural pattern books grow into a truly mass-market-phenomenon.

Romantic Revival Interiors

The pattern books written by Andrew Jackson Downing and his contemporaries depart significantly from the earlier builders' guides in their specifications for interiors. Before the 1840s, consumers outside large cities had few sources to turn to in their search for information about interior decoration, but by the middle of the nineteenth century, home builders could rely on pattern books for counsel. Downing's *Cottage Residences* (1842) devoted some space to a discussion of the convenient arrangement of interiors, with emphasis on the value of closets, pantries, and well-ventilated bedrooms. In *The Architecture of Country Houses* (1850), he made interiors a major theme, with a lengthy chapter devoted to "Interior Finishing of Country Houses" and another on "Furniture." The text abounds with comments about decoration and paint colors, window curtains, and chimney pieces.

The Architecture of Country Houses offers some of the few contemporary published images from which builders and their clients could learn about fashionable interiors; pre–Civil War books by Gervase Wheeler, Samuel Sloan, and Calvert Vaux contain no illustrations of interiors. This may explain why Joseph Revere

Fig. 86. In The Architecture of Country Houses, *A. J. Downing was the only pattern-book author of the period to publish significant interior views.*

Fig. 87. The flambeau finial above the library mantel is consistent with Gothic ornament throughout The Willows.

Fig. 88. Downing's design for a Tudor-arched fireplace illustrates his attempt to reproduce historically correct architectural details.

and his talented carpenter-builder, Ashbel Bruen, turned to Downing for ideas when they created the interior of The Willows. Although its exterior was built nearly line for line from a design in *Rural Homes* (see Fig. 52), Wheeler's book offered only floor plans and a few written references to the appearance of rooms. But in *Country Houses*, Downing's illustrations for a Gothic bedroom and a Gothic parlor both bear a remarkable resemblance to rooms at The Willows.

Revere and Bruen seem to have adapted the "Interior in a simple Gothic Style" (Downing's parlor) for the library. Downing's engraving (Fig. 86) depicts a room with two projecting bay windows and a fireplace. The placement of windows and fireplace corresponds to those features in Revere's library, although the window opposite the fireplace at The Willows does not extend to the floor, as it does in the engraving. Revere's black marble mantel is in the same Tudor-arched style that Downing illustrated, a type readily available in stoneworkers' shops in Newark and New York. The wooden Tudor arch with flambeau finial above the mantel (Fig. 87) comes directly from Downing's succeeding illustration, "Drawing Room at Kenwood, Gothic Style" (Fig. 88).

The parlor engraving depicts one bay with a Tudor-arched window and the other with a square-headed window. At The Willows both windows are square-headed, as preferred by Downing. In *Country Houses* he wrote, "To our own feeling there is more *domesticity* in the square-headed window, and we would therefore only introduce the arch, in the doors and windows of private houses, in particular cases, when the stronger indication of style is needed to give spirit to the composition."

On the second floor of The Willows Downing's influence is even more telling. There, the two principal bedrooms incorporate curved ceilings, described by Wheeler as "being lathed upon the curved beams that support the roof." But it is only Downing, in an engraving in *Country Houses*, who shows the pattern-book reader how such a treatment looks (Fig. 89).

Although Downing's "Bed-room in the Gothic Style" depicts an angular rather than a barrel-vaulted ceiling, the exposed beams, their placement, and the location of the end-wall window all correspond to the appearance of two bedrooms at The Willows. Downing also recommends "showing about half the depth of the real beams of the ceiling, plastering as usual between, and placing bold brackets underneath them along the cornice of the room." Cast in plaster and painted to imitate wood, just such bold brackets are still in place beneath the exposed beams in these bedrooms (Fig. 90).

Downing acknowledged that the illustration for the Gothic bedroom came from a drawing by his friend, the architect Alexander Jackson Davis. Davis's drawing depicted a bedroom he had remodeled in his mother's house, "Kerri Cottage," which stood on

Warren Street in Newark. Though Kerri Cottage has long since been demolished, Davis's early experiments with a Gothic Revival interior survive at The Willows, through the translation of original architecture to pattern book, and then back to built form through the efforts of Joseph Revere and Ashbel Bruen.

Fig. 89. The "Interior of a bedroom in the Gothic style" appeared in Downing's second pattern book, The Architecture of Country Houses

Fig. 90. The brackets or corbels in the bedrooms at The Willows match those in Downing's illustrations (see Figs. 86 and 88).

3

NEW TECHNOLOGIES, NEW STYLES

Steam, Timber, and Nails

Gleaming with scarlet paint and gilt flourishes, the mighty Corliss engine whirred and throbbed like some idol of the future. From the day the Centennial Exposition opened on May 10, 1876, crowds thronged the Engineering Hall to see this wonder. The miraculous power of steam was changing the nation: steam-driven locomotives had closed unbridgeable distances; steam had replaced water power and brute muscle as the motive force in sawmills and textile mills; planers, routers, lathes and jigsaws—all powered by steam—had revolutionized architecture; and steam-powered printing presses were bringing more newspapers and books to more readers than ever before.

Not the least of these books were architectural pattern books. They heralded a revolution in building that relied to a large extent on an innovation almost as important as steam machinery, one that began in Chicago just as steam was asserting its power. Chicago in the mid-1830s was a boom town. Its demand for new housing was far outstripping the potential of the ancient braced-frame construction method when some native genius invented an unprecedented construction technique.[1] Nearly overnight it reduced dramatically the time, money, and skill necessary to erect a building. Dubbed the "balloon" frame by scoffers who predicted its instant collapse in a stiff wind, the new frame proved all of its critics fools. Instead of massive timbers joined together painstakingly with mortise-and-tenon joints, the balloon frame was an airy basketwork of light, machine-cut lumber nailed together with cheap, machine-made nails (Fig. 91).

In Chicago the balloon frame was an instant success. According to one observer, "If it had not been for the knowledge of balloon frames, Chicago and San Francisco would never have arisen as

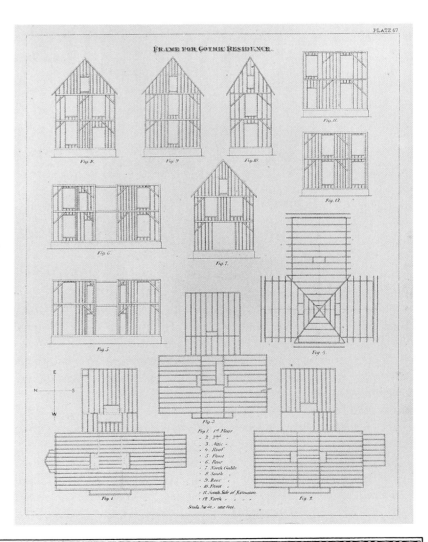

Fig. 91. The balloon frame and Romantic Revival architecture developed concurrently. A. J. Bicknell's Detail, Cottage, and Constructive Architecture *of 1873 illustrated how a Gothic-style house could be built with a balloon frame. (Avery Architectural and Fine Arts Library, Columbia University in the City of New York)*

Fig. 92. When the 1795 sanctuary of the First Presbyterian Church of Morristown was dismantled in 1893, its heavy mortise-and-tenon frame was revealed. Braced-frame construction was the standard structural system for all wooden buildings before the balloon frame. (Joint Free Public Library of Morristown and Morris Township)

they did, from little villages to great cities in a single year."[2] Back east, where demand was lighter and builders were more conservative (Fig. 92), the new technique took a while to gain favor. Its first appearance in New Jersey has not been documented, but some carpenter-builders, like Ashbel Bruen, who built The Willows in 1853 (see Fig. 50) had accepted it by midcentury, although even then its use was not universal. The frontispiece from Edward Shaw's *The Modern Architect* (1855) confirms the modernity of the title by illustrating a balloon-frame barn under construction next to a just-completed and very up-to-date-looking house. Gathered around a top-hatted architect or builder is a group of "mechanics" ready to translate the spread-out plans to built form with their simple hand tools (Fig. 93). As if to underscore the ease of the balloon-frame method, even the workers are attired in waistcoats, dress shirts, and ties. The very fervor with which pattern books of the 1860s continued to extol the balloon frame's virtues proved that some skeptical builders still needed reassurance. One outspoken partisan was George E. Woodward, who in 1865 claimed that "a man and a boy can now attain the same results, with ease, that twenty men could on an old-fashioned frame." Woodward went on to insist that "old-fogy builders who are averse to learning anything new, are yielding to a belief in its merits."[3]

Fig. 93. Modern style, in the form of a house with brackets and veranda, and modern technology, in the form of a balloon frame, were both illustrated in this 1855 engraving. (Avery Architectural and Fine Arts Library, Columbia University in the City of New York)

From the start, everyone admitted the economics of the balloon frame: cheaper and faster construction with fewer skilled hands. As it became a standard technique, however, a subtler result became evident: the new framing method was changing not only the construction but the appearance of architecture. Combined with the uniformity of standardized machine-cut lumber, the balloon frame contributed a sense of precision and clarity. It made the outline of a house more easily perceived as a thin, crisp curtain rather than as a cumbersome structure needed to support a roof (Fig. 94). In addition, the new system encouraged flexible planning and prompted architects to experiment with the asymmetrical massing that expressed Romantic ideals so vividly.[4]

Conditions in New Jersey after the Civil War were ripe for

Fig. 94. (opposite) Elisha Hussey's 1876 pattern book, Home Building, illustrated a typical mid-nineteenth-century house, built in Hackensack by a carpenter named Samuel Fink. Its thin-walled construction was possible because of the balloon frame.

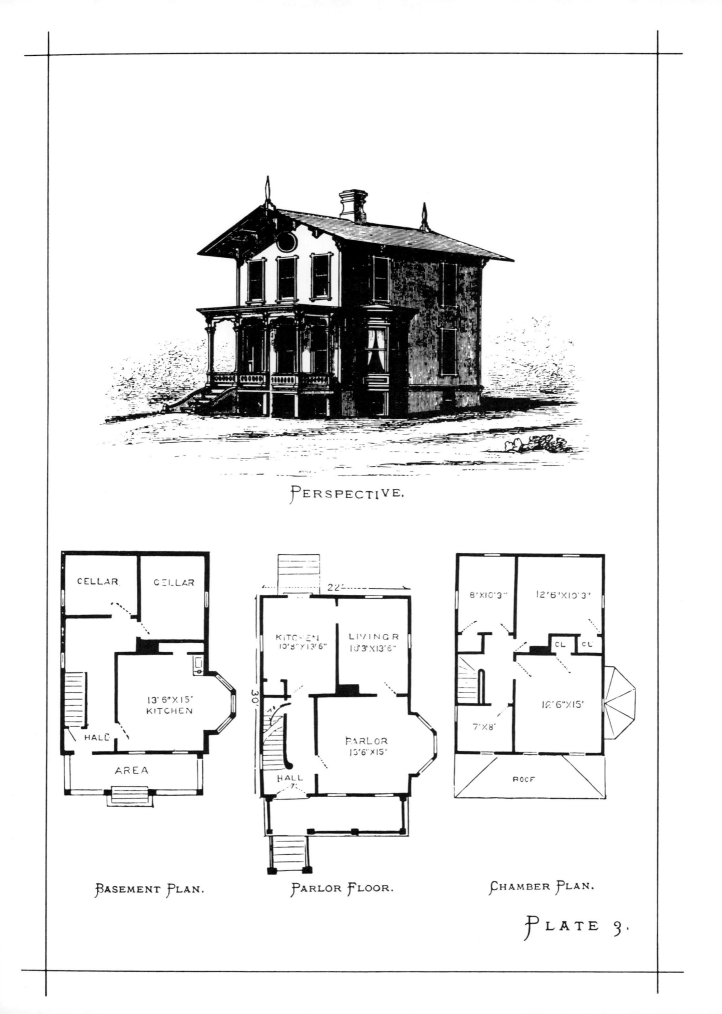

PERSPECTIVE.

BASEMENT PLAN.

CELLAR CELLAR

13'6"X15' KITCHEN

HALL

AREA

PARLOR FLOOR.

22'

KITCHEN 10'3"Y13'6"

LIVING R 10'3"X13'6"

30'

PARLOR 13'6"X15'

HALL 7'

CHAMBER PLAN.

8'X10'3"

12'6"X10'3"

CL CL

12'6"X15'

7'X8'

ROOF

PLATE 3.

these new possibilities. In the town of Boonton in northern Morris County's iron belt the largest nail factory in the United States thundered away,[5] pouring out cheap and perfectly uniform cut nails by the ton. (Fig. 95). Thanks to better rail connections, lumberyards were no longer tied to sawmill sites; almost every community with a railroad spur and a freight depot boasted its own lumberyard, often with a millwork shop attached, where window sash, doors, and miles of molding and trim were produced (Fig. 96). Sawmills themselves, once bound to water power, could be built anywhere, thanks to steam.

Technical and artistic innovation did not invariably proceed in tandem. Decades before technological advances had equaled architectural inspiration, innovators and traditionalists found themselves at loggerheads. Writing in 1837 about the construction of an avant-garde Gothic Revival house, one critic complained that "the novelty of the style met with much opposition from the mechanics employed, and, in occasionally yielding to their opinions, the char-

Fig. 95. The "Nail Makers" referred to the inhabitants of the industrial town of Boonton in northern New Jersey. Harper's New Monthly Magazine *published a feature-length article about the Boonton Iron Works in its July 1860 issue. (General Research Division, The New York Public Library, Astor, Lenox and Tilden Foundations)*

Fig. 96. William Blanchard established his "turning mill" in Bloomingdale in 1888. In conjunction with his sawmill he produced the kind of ornament that characterized domestic architecture during the second half of the nineteenth century. (Photo from Historic Bloomingdale by Emil Salvini, © 1984 Colorama Historic Publications. Used with permission of the author)

acter of the building was in some measure injured."[6] Although the architectural pattern books of the 1850s advocated stylistic innovation and later pattern books introduced important technical innovation house building remained a conservative craft for decades longer. Despite the widespread acceptance of the balloon frame and other improvements, carpenters, masons, painters, and plasterers (Fig. 97) often felt beleaguered by new materials and new methods—especially steam-powered machinery. In self-protection they perpetuated the methods of their forebears whenever circumstances permitted—one reason that so many pattern-book designs were executed in simplified form. Tension between workers and entrepreneurs is suggested by William Ranlett, who, in *The Architect*, grumbled about carpenters who tried to learn on the job without a proper apprenticeship. But workers were often no happier: between 1833 and 1837, carpenters in northeastern cities went on strike thirty-four times.[7] Minard Lafever sounded like an arbiter of this disquiet when he wrote in 1839 in *The Beauties of Modern Architecture*:

Fig. 97. Ambrotype portraits of now anonymous workmen illustrate three important nineteenth-century trades: plastering, carpentry, and painting. (Collection of Bates and Isabel Lowry)

Fig. 98. James P. Goltra of Bernards Township was a master builder active during the first half of the nineteenth century, when technological and stylistic changes transformed American domestic architecture.

PRICES OF BUILDING MATERIALS AND LABOR,

AT NEW YORK, JANUARY, 1869.

Estimates in this work are based on the prices here given, and cost of erection in other localities will be fixed by the local prices of materials.

MASON WORK AND MATERIALS.
Stone wall, including all materials, laid dry, per foot 23 cents.
do   do laid with mortar,   -   -   do 23 do.
Excavation, per cubic yard,   -   -   -   40 do.
Brick, per thousand, laid. Pale, $19 50 to $23 50. Hard burned, $21 to $25.
Cement, per barrel, $2 50 to $3.
Lime,   do $1 75.
Hair, per bushel,   70 cents.
Lath and plastering, including all materials, 1 coat, per square yard, 40 cents.
    do   do   do   2 coats,   do   60 do.
    do   do   do   3 coats,   do   70 do.
Laths, per thousand, $3 50 to $4 50.

Prices for all the timber, covering, flooring and finishing lumber, per thousand feet, board measure.

FRAMING TIMBER.
Pine, $45. Sawed to order. Spruce, $25. Sawed to order.
Hemlock, $22 to $25.
Firring, 2 inches wide, 6 cents each.
Studding, 13 feet by 2 × 4 inches, 21 cents each. 3 × 4, 24 cents each.
Shingles, $8 to $10.

ROOFING.
Hemlock, 1 inch thick $24 per thousand.
Pine, 1¼ inches thick, matched, $45 per thousand.
Spruce,   do   do $35   do
Slating, per square of 100 feet, metal extra. 1st quality of slates, $15. 2d quality, $14.
Tinning, per square of 100 feet, $11 to $13.
Leaders, 4 inches calibre, per lineal foot, 30 cents.

FLOORING.
Spruce, 5 inches wide, 1¼-inch thick, $35 per thousand, planed and matched.
Spruce, 10 inches wide, 1¼-inch thick, planed and matched, $35 per thousand,
White pine, 5 inches wide, as above, $45.
White pine, 10 inches wide, as above, $45.
Georgia pine, 3 to 5 inches wide, $60 to $80, 1¼-inch thick, planed and matched.
Hemlock, 1-inch thick, matched, $24.

FINISHING STOCK, SEASONED.
Clear white pine, $65 per thousand.
Second quality of clear pine, $40 to $50.

HARDWARE.
Nails, per cwt., $5 75.

LABOR PER DAY.
Stone Mason, $4 00.   Mason's Tender, $3 00.
Bricklayer,   5 00.   Carpenter,   3 75.
Plasterer,   5 50.   Painter,   3 50.   Laborer, $2 00.

x

Fig. 99. A table for "time and materials," still a common way of figuring construction costs, was drawn up for the New York area in a pattern book published in 1869.

Notwithstanding the many works which have heretofore been published on the subject of Architecture, there has none yet appeared intended exclusively for the operative workman. It is therefore thought proper to present to the industrious and ingenious, a book . . . which will enable him to become a complete master of his business, more systematically than by any other plan yet adopted, and more particularly so, *when studied in connection with his practical pursuits* [emphasis added].

The tradition-bound nature of the building trades is reflected in contemporary sources, which record skills transmitted from generation to generation. Typical of builders trained before midcentury was James P. Goltra (Fig. 98), a Somerset County, New Jersey, master carpenter who died in 1871 at the age of seventy nine, a decade before the first American carpenters' union was chartered. A local biography recounted that "his father was a carpenter and builder and brought up his son to that occupation, who followed it as his chief business til towards the close of his life, building extensively and erecting many churches in Bernard and adjoining townships."[8] Wondrous steam-powered gadgets notwithstanding, it was the skilled master builder like Goltra, and the unskilled laborer, who remained the backbone of New Jersey building, whether working from traditional sources or pattern-book inspiration. Wages for the various building trades and costs for materials were specified in George Woodward's 1869 pattern book, *The National Architect*. Published in New York, its prices pertained in most of New Jersey as well (Fig. 99).

Octagonal Walls Built to Last

Because the United States has always been a wood-building nation, advances in masonry construction were few before the radical change in building size at the beginning of the twentieth century. In the history of American masonry construction, however, one pattern book stands out for its innovative content. In 1848 Orson Squire Fowler published *A Home for All*, a book suffused with rationalism inspired by faith in the potential of technology. Fowler's thesis was simple: the circle was the most efficient way to enclose the most space, but circular houses were difficult to build. Closest to the circle was the octagon, which offered cheaper construction cost per square foot of livable space than did conventional house shapes—or so Fowler claimed. Not only that, it provided light and air from every direction (important health considerations for nineteenth-century builders), and in its center core utilities could be clustered efficiently; far ahead of his time, Fowler advocated indoor plumbing, central heating and dumbwaiters as essential equipment for the ordinary, middle-class house. His floor plans did not call for pie-shaped rooms, but dedicated the odd angles created by the octagon shape to closets and other subsidiary uses (Fig. 100).

In 1853 Fowler brought out a heavily revised edition of *A Home for All*. As the result of having been introduced to a "new" material

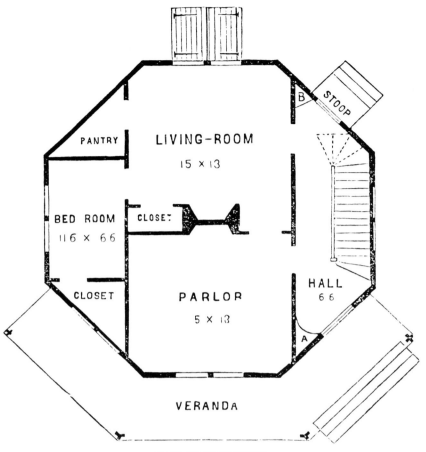

PLAN OF FIRST STORY.

Fig. 100. With a basement kitchen and ample closets throughout, the octagon provided larger ground floor rooms theoretically free of clutter and cooking odors.

(in reality one used in ancient Rome), he subtitled this edition *The Gravel Wall and Octagon Mode of Building.* Fowler had grown convinced that the "gravel wall" was the most economical and durable material available. A kind of concrete, it was made of water and lime mixed with sand and gravel from the building site. Fowler poured his mixture into wooden forms and cured one course at a time until the desired building height was reached. Finally, he covered the walls with stucco to create a smooth finish.

Gravel-wall octagons sprang up from Maine to Maryland as Fowler spread the good word with effective self-promotion. His own impressive octagonal house in Fishkill, New York, inspired a concentration of octagons in the Hudson River Valley. Two of the earliest octagonal houses in New Jersey built according to Fowler's specifications contemplate one another from either side of the same street in the iron town of Boonton. One was built by Nathaniel Myers and the other by G.V.S. Rickards a year after the revised edition of *A Home for All* was published; both houses do Fowler one better in their use of site-specific materials. Instead of gravel, Myers and Rickards added bits of slag from the iron foundry where they worked, creating a super-durable reinforced concrete. The better preserved of the two is the house built by Rickards (Fig. 101). Its porch, cupola, and bracketed eaves are consistent with the simple Italianate features that Fowler preferred.

Not all New Jersey builders chose to combine the octagonal shape with the innovative gravel-wall material. When Ira J. Lindsley built "Fordville" in Hanover Township for the prosperous farmer Edwin Ford in 1857–58, he followed Fowler's instructions for poured concrete, but instead of building an octagon he used the material for a traditional rectangular house that ignored the architectural fashions of the day. Family records prove that Lindsley owned *A Home for All*, along with the 1854 edition of Asher Benjamin's 1830 book, *The Practical House Carpenter*, and Gervase Wheeler's *Homes for the People*, just published in 1858.[9] The mix-

Fig. 101. When George Rickards built his octagonal house in 1854 he used the plan and gravel-wall construction method advanced in Orson Fowler's 1853 book, A Home for All.

Fig. 102. The clearest example of how buildings were influenced by published sources is the octagon house. Built all over New Jersey, its only source is Fowler's book. *This example stands in Cape May.*

Fig. 103. "The Octagon Cottage," in an elevation drawing published in Fowler's A Home for All.

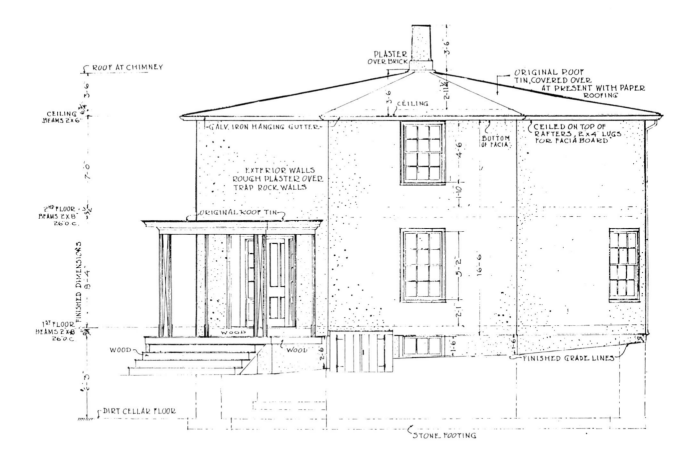

Fig. 104. John Gibbs mimicked the external appearance of Fowler's gravel wall by coating rubblestone with stucco. His octagon house represents the transition from regional vernacular architecture to a common "American" architecture promoted by published sources. (Historic American Buildings Survey)

ture of old and new in his library as well as in his work made Lindsley typical of the builders of his generation. Ira's traditional bent may have been encouraged by his father Joseph, builder of the Morris County Courthouse (see Fig. 18). Whether Ira might have adopted a more contemporary outlook with maturity is impossible to say. In 1862 he became captain of Company C of the 15th Regiment, New Jersey Volunteers. A year later he was killed in the Battle of Chancellorsville near Fredericksburg, Virginia.

In an approach exactly opposite to Lindsley's, many New Jersey builders rejected the gravel-wall method but embraced the octagonal shape. One such wooden octagon stands in Montvale; another, in Cape May (Fig. 102), looks as if its builder lifted it directly from the pages of a *A Home for All* (Fig. 103). A traditional material other than wood is found in the rural village of Johnsonburg in Warren County, where in 1853 John C. Gibbs built a Fowler octagon of locally available trap rock, with a stuccoed finish (Fig. 104).

Although relatively few octagonal houses were built in New Jersey, the octagon shape proved more popular than Fowler's

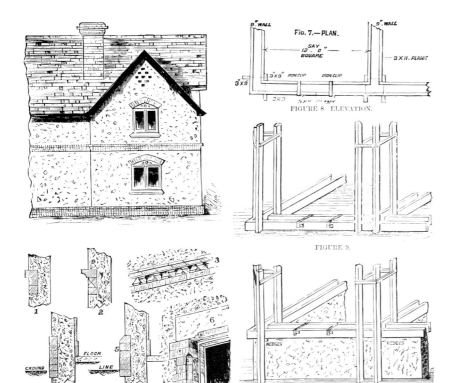

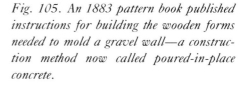

Fig. 105. An 1883 pattern book published instructions for building the wooden forms needed to mold a gravel wall—a construction method now called poured-in-place concrete.

Fig. 106. In 1887 the traditional-looking laundry building at The Hermitage was constructed using the innovative gravel-wall method of construction. The structurally conservative but stylistically innovative house it served was remodeled in 1847–1848 by William Ranlett.

Orson Squire Fowler

The fad for octagonal houses, one of mid-nineteenth-century America's most curious architectural byways, was promoted by one of the era's oddest characters. Orson Squire Fowler (1809–1887), publisher, author, and social reformer, promoted every radical idea current at midcentury—universal suffrage, abolition, mesmerism, dress reform, hydrotherapy, vegetarianism, and sexual science. A self-proclaimed expert at phrenology, the "science" of reading character through bumps on the skull (*right*), Fowler founded *The American Phrenological Journal*. In New York City he opened a phrenological practice, where his many eminent subjects included Walt Whitman, who incorporated some of Fowler's phrenological vocabulary into his poetry. All of Fowler's books dealt with some aspect of human health and happiness: *Love and Parentage Applied to the Improvement of Offspring*; *Marriage, Its History and Philosophy*; *Matrimony, or Phrenology and Physiology Applied to the Selection of Congenial Companions for Life*; and the nearly one-thousand-page *Sexual Science*. Committed to practicing what he preached, Fowler's personal research was abetted by three marriages.

His interest in architecture grew out of these same concerns for health and the importance of a well-ordered family environment. Fowler published the first edition of *A Home for All* in 1848. Soon after he was introduced to the gravel-wall method of construction he enthusiastically incorporated that technology into a thoroughly revised edition of *A Home for All* in 1853.

Some of Fowler's pursuits, especially phrenology, impress us today as charlatanism. Viewed in the context of their time, however, all of his interests reflect a faith in rationalism, science, and social reform typical of the 1850s, no matter how naive the placement of that faith may seem more

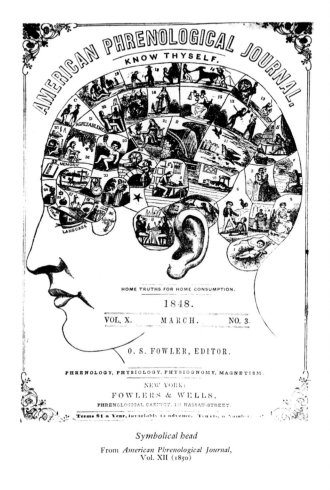

Symbolical head
From *American Phrenological Journal*,
Vol. XII (1850)

than a century later. His candor about human sexuality, his fascination with the presumed scientific basis of character traits, and his dedication to a "home for all" based on practical technology bespeak faith in the scientific method and the American idea of Progress. Fowler's success at all of these endeavors was made possible by another typically American talent that was flexing its muscles at midcentury—self-promotion.

Brackets

"Brackets ubiquitous! Brackets indispensable!" might have been the slogan of any pattern-book author of the second half of the nineteenth century. Andrew Jackson Downing put such stock in their importance that an entire bracketed mode emerged from his work, a manner of building that became typically American, eventually growing into a style known popularly as Hudson River Bracketed. Integral to the Italianate style, brackets added weight and solidity to nearly every towered and cubical Italianate villa design. Often set in pairs under deeply projecting eaves, brackets reached a height of four to five feet and contributed to the dramatic chiarascuro effects of Italianate cornices.

In its Franco-Italianate dress, the Second Empire style offered a gorgeous array of bracketed cornices, bracketed windows and doors, and bracketed porches. Garnished with acanthus leaves and drop pendants (*right*), the mass-produced, curvaceous brackets of the Second Empire house were a striking adverstisement for the efficiency of American steam-powered woodworking machinery in the service of architectural delight.

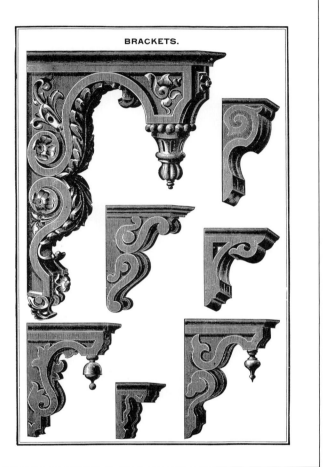

BRACKETS.

concrete construction method, which never came close to supplanting the newly popular balloon frame. But enough interest survived in alternative materials for Robert Shoppell to revive the gravel-wall method in 1883. In *How to Build, Furnish, and Decorate*, Shoppell presented Fowler's technique (without credit) as one ideally suited to the construction of outbuildings (Fig. 105). It was from this source that the builders of the laundry at The Hermitage in Ho-Ho-Kus took their inspiration (Fig. 106). Because the gravel aggregate is so large, the laundry building's walls look almost like rubblestone construction with wide joints, but since the exterior was never finished with stucco the marks of the wooden forms are still visible.[10] Although limited in its application during his lifetime, Fowler's method was an important precursor of early-twentieth-century experiments with poured and reinforced concrete construction.

The French Roof Craze

Far more agreeable to American builders than the strictly geometrical octagon were styles that capitalized on the inherent flexibility of wooden construction. The first new style to coincide with the popular acceptance of the balloon frame was the Second Empire style. Often called the "Modern French style" in its day, it swept across New Jersey in the late 1860s and early 1870s with an *a la mode* appeal rivaled only by enthusiasm for the latest in Parisian couture. Writing in 1868, Samuel Sloan was clearly among the converted: "The French Roof—or, as it is often called, the Mansard—was and is in great request. Public and private dwellings, and even stables, are covered with this new roof; and no man who wants a fashionable house will be without it." French Roof frenzy reached such a pitch that according to one newspaper, "A short time ago no one seemed to know that buildings had roofs. . . . Suddenly, however, a sort of roof epidemic seized us, and now no building, great or small, can be a building without its French roof."[11]

In keeping with the building campaigns of Napoleon III, which had created the vogue for French architecture in the United States, the most impressive American interpretations of the Second Empire style were public buildings. Only ambitious undertakings like Alfred B. Mullett's State War and Navy Building (1871–1875) and Philadelphia City Hall by John McArthur, Jr. (begun 1874), could echo the sculptural richness and plasticity of their Parisian models. For residential architecture, it was usually nothing more than the unmistakable mansard roof that identified an American

Fig. 107. A photograph of Clinton Street in Trenton shows the coexistence of Italianate and Second Empire houses in a fashionable neighborhood of the 1870s. (Trenton Public Library, Trentoniana Collection)

house as Second Empire; massing and details were borrowed from the Italianate, with console brackets and facade towers among the more common features. This combination of Franco-Italianate elements was responsible for the appearance of entire New Jersey neighborhoods after the Civil War (Fig. 107).

Although no single architect-author spoke as forcefully for the Second Empire style as A. J. Downing had for the Gothic and Italianate, several pattern-book writers were instrumental in promoting the mansardic house. The books of Marcus Fayette Cummings and Charles Crosby Miller were among the most influential. Their first pattern book, *Architecture*, published in 1865, was notable for its large format and clear line drawings of porches, window moldings, and door enframements (Fig. 108). The popularity of *Architecture* is proven by the number of its details that can be found on New Jersey houses of the 1860s and 1870s (Fig. 109).

Even more closely associated with New Jersey was A. J. Bicknell, who published his own designs and those of others. *Bicknell's Village Builder and Supplement* (1878) was full of plans and elevations for Second Empire townhouses, suburban houses, town halls, and schools. It was a summation of the style's popularity published just when that popularity was beginning to wane. Although Bicknell's was a New York City publishing imprint, many of the designs in his books were created by D. B. Provoost, T. Thompson, and C. Graham & Son, all architects who practiced in Elizabeth, New Jersey. Provoost's design for a three-bay mansarded dwelling (Fig. 110) is a model for innumerable New Jersey houses. Its popularity no doubt resulted from its marriage of current architectural fashion with the conventional and easily built side-hall plan familiar since its depiction by Asher Benjamin at the opening of the nineteenth century. Provoost's illustration displays richly modeled elliptically arched windows, a pronounced concave roof, and deep

Fig. 108. Detail of a dormer window from Architecture, *published by Cummings and Miller in 1865.*

Fig. 109. Dormer window from an ambitious Second Empire house in Bound Brook.

eaves, all marks of the late phase of the style. A realization of his design, perfect down to every detail, stands not far from the Somerset County Courthouse in Somerville (Fig. 111). It includes all the features to be found in a solidly middle-class version of the Second Empire house: tall ground-floor windows sheltered by a porch carried on chamfered posts that terminate with flat brackets; an arched double-leaf door with glass upper panels; a wide frieze, here decorated with a scalloped molding instead of panels; tripled brackets beneath a deep cornice; dormer windows; and a heavy wooden curb at the top of the roof. Only the metal cresting has vanished.

Sometime around 1875 in Millburn, the Pettigrew family posed for the photographer on the porch of their mansard house (Fig. 112). At first glance it seems identical to the house in Somerville. A closer look reveals a far more pedestrian version of the three-bay side-hall type, with stiff, flat brackets, a shallow cornice, and none of the distinctive window trim found in Provoost's design. The Pettigrew house reveals how easily the Second Empire could be reduced to a surface style, far removed from the high-style models that were its inspiration.

Larger Second Empire houses usually incorporated some version of the tower inherited from Downing's classic Italianate villa design (see Fig. 48). "The addition of a *Tower* does not add greatly to the expense . . . while the room at the top makes a good observatory." So advised the *American Agriculturist* in its March 1869 edition, as part of a lengthy description of "A Very Complete Country House" (Fig. 113), giving the lie to the assumption that the Second Empire was invariably an urban style. One New Jersey version of this elaborate design survives in Hackettstown, a country location even today. The exterior displays absolute fidelity to the published engraving. Tripled and bull's eye windows and a chevron-motif frieze are unusual tower enrichments (Fig. 114). The house also features lacy iron cresting along the top of the roof, ornament typical of the Second Empire house but absent from the *Agriculturist's* illustration.

Several designers proposed a house with a plan and three-bay elevation similar to the *American Agriculturist* version, but with the tower truncated to become no more than a projecting center pavilion. By the 1880s few builders remained enamored of the Second Empire style, although Robert Shoppell persevered with a masonry version of the center-pavilion type (Fig. 115) in his 1883 book, *How to Build, Furnish, and Decorate*. One of many houses like it, but executed in wood, can be found in Morristown (Fig. 116).

Although the style is most frequently associated with moderate to large-size houses, pattern-book authors did publish designs for more modest versions. Relatively uncommon when compared to the larger Second Empire house, but obviously appealing to

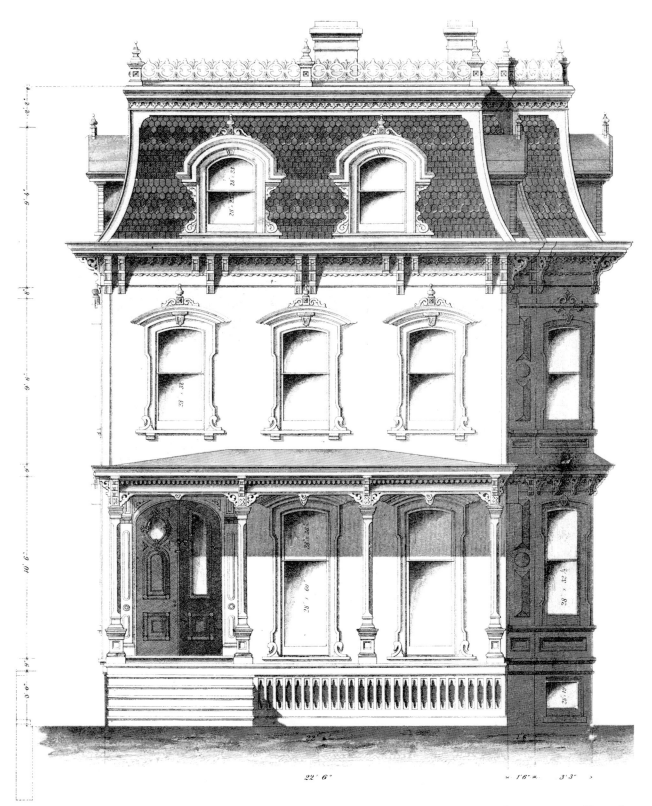

SUPPLEMENTARY PLATE 1

Fig. 110. (opposite) *Originally published in color, "Supplemental Plate One" from* Bicknell's Village Builder *exerted a powerful influence on domestic architecture in New Jersey.*

Fig. 111. Few versions of the three-bay Second Empire house were built with such fidelity to Bicknell's Village Builder *plate as this one in Somerville.*

some builders, was the one-story mansard-roofed cottage. In Vineland one such cottage (Fig. 117) resembles an engraving from *Woodward's Country Homes* (Fig. 118), shorn of its porch. A similar house in Metuchen (Fig. 119) is a variant of a design from *Bicknell's Village Builder* (Fig. 120), a design that the pattern-book notes could be built for $1,500 in 1878. Fine examples of the mansarded

Fig. 112. A photograph of the Pettigrew house and its occupants documents the impact of industry on post–Civil War society. The jigsawn brackets framing the porch, the bricks in the chimney, the chairs on the porch, and the family's clothes were all mass-produced. (Millburn-Short Hills Historical Society)

cottage can be found in Boonton, Plainfield, and Summit. In some places a flurry of Second Empire popularity can be detected in the development pattern of an entire neighborhood. In the St. Cloud section of West Orange, for example, three Second Empire cottages stand in the shadow of half a dozen larger Second Empire houses, making the mansarded house the dominant type in the neighborhood.

The cottage variant was not the only Second Empire curiosity. As if to confound future architectural historians, pattern-book authors also put great stock in the mansard roof as an easy and distinctive method of modernizing older houses, so the roof alone is not always a foolproof dating device. One unusually well-documented mansard modernization typical of many is the Ichabod Compton, Jr., house, in Mauricetown. Built in 1812 in the Federal style by Flagg Bacon, a carpenter and carver of unusual ability, it was converted to a Second Empire double house (Fig. 121) in 1883 by Griffith Pritchard, a local builder.[12]

Fig. 114. This complex Second Empire house was created by a master builder working from a few simple floor plans and elevation drawings published in the American Agriculturalist.

Fig. 113. One of the largest-circulation magazines of the last quarter of the nineteenth century was the American Agriculturalist, which published a house design monthly; its back pages carried advertisements for popular pattern books.

Fig. 115. Until the Colonial Revival, the Second Empire was the last of the nineteenth century's styles firmly grounded in classical architecture.

Fig. 116. Unlike the curved and flared roof-lines of the best high-style examples, the mansard roof of this Second Empire house is straight and stiff.

Fig. 117. Vineland, the home of this man-sarded cottage, was created by James K. Landis in 1861, just as the Second Empire style was becoming popular in America. Landis sold inexpensive building lots in hopes of developing a picturesque and healthy community for working women and men.

Fig. 118. George Woodward, architect, developer, and pattern-book author, offered this design for a mansard-roofed cottage in his 1865 book, Woodward's Country Homes. He called it an ideal suburban house for a family of moderate means.

Although not a major variant numerically, one final variation on the French style deserves mention because its source remains puzzling. In some ways the most plastic of the residential Second Empire types, this version displays a facade animated not by a tower or central pavilion but by a pair of two-story bays that frame the entrance. A masonry example in Hopewell (Fig. 122) and a frame version in Roselle (Fig. 123) are nearly identical but for their materials. The distinctiveness of the type and its wide distribution throughout the state (from the Queen Victoria Inn in Cape May to a house in South Plainfield) argue for a published source, but that source has so far eluded identification. Design V from

Fig. 119. Photographed in 1932, this simple pattern-book cottage had changed little since its construction in the 1880s. (Metuchen-Edison Historical Society)

Hobbs's Architecture, "to be built on the bank of the Raritan River at New Brunswick by Dr. Robbins," looks as if it might be two-thirds of this house type. Design XXIX (Fig. 124) is also similar. Isaac Hobbs's identity as the designer of many houses published in *Godey's Lady's Book* points to his authorship of an exact prototype for the Roselle and Hopewell houses.

Despite the Panic of 1873, which stalled construction nationwide just at the peak of the Second Empire style's popularity, the building trades and the French style recovered before the end of the decade, insuring that mansard roofs would remain a feature of the suburban landscape for another ten years, although with steadily diminishing impact. Pattern-book support for the Second Empire style generated an uncounted number of mansard houses in New Jersey; except for those few unusually ambitious examples that were architect-designed, every one was indebted to a published source in some way and at some remove.

The Second Empire style was waning, but at the same time pattern books were reaching a broader audience. The technological improvements in house-building and domestic comforts that pattern books furthered were growing more commonplace as they became more innovative. Stylistically, the residual classicism and restraint of the Second Empire house was about to give way to a frenzy of architectural eclecticism. New Jersey was ready for a bold new chapter in the pattern-book story.

Residential MLS #: 3172251   **Status:** Active   **LP:** $485,000

308 Aurora St Hudson, OH 44236-2940   **SP:**

Subdivision/Complex: **Closing Date:**

Property Subtype: Single Family   **County:** Summit

Parcel ID #: 3201158   **Multiple PIN #'s:** No

Area: SUM14   **MLS Cross Ref #:**

Photos: 25   **VT:**

Directions: Rt. 91 N (Main Street) to Hudson Aurora Street. House on south side of Aurora St.

Single Family   **Maint. Fee:** $0 /   **Unit Floor #:** 0   **Unit Location:**

Maint.Incl:

Restrictions:

Property Information	**Approx Fin SqFt:** 3900	**Annual Taxes:** $6,160	**School Dist:** Hudson CSD
# Bedrooms: 4	SqFt Source: Owner	House Faces: North	Disability Features: No
# Baths: 4 (3 1)	Lot Size: 0.459 acres	Exterior: Vinyl	Warranty: No
# Rooms: 10	Lot Size Source: Public Record Auto	Roof: Asphalt/Fiberglass	Fixer Upper: No
# Fireplaces: 3	Lot frontage/Depth: 100 x 200	Year Built: 1959	Public Trans:
# Stories: 2 Story	Irregular: No	Construction:	Avail for Auction: No
Style: Colonial		Dwelling Type: Detached	Auction Date/Time:
HOA: No		Incl:	

Basement: Finished,Unfinished

Heating Type: Forced Air   **Fence:**

Cooling Type: Central Air   **Heating Fuel:** Gas

Garage # of Cars: 2   **Driveway:** Paved   **Water/Sewer:** Public Sewer,Public Water

Garage Features: Attached,Door Opener,Drain,Electric,Heated

Exterior Features: Deck,Porch

Lot Description: Wooded/Treed

View Description: Wooded

Appliances/Equip: Dishwasher,Garbage Disposal,Microwave,Oven,Range,Refrigerator,Security System,Smoke Detector,Sump Pump

Amenities:

Room Name	Dim	Lvl	Wnd Trtmt	Fireplace	Flooring	Full Bath Level: Upper	Half Bath Level: Main
Great Room	19x28	First			Wood		
Living	15x23	First			Wood		
Family							
Kitchen	15x14	First			Wood		
Dining	15x12	First			Wood		
Mstr Bed	20x13	Second			Wood		
Bed # 2	17x11	Second			Wood		
Bed # 3	14x14	Second			Wood		
Bed # 4	14x11	Second			Wood		
Office	14x14	First			Wood		

(handwritten: 4-5 I BOX. Side)

Miscellaneous Rooms: Eat-in Kitchen,Foyer,Master Bath,Office

Remarks: Stately 4 BR, 3 1/2 bath colonial located in the heart of Hudson! This home of timeless elegance is situated on a picturesque lot w/mature trees & landscaping. Center hall foyer w/slate floors opens to spacious rooms throughout! Charming 1st floor library w/woodburning fireplace, hardwood floors & wall of built-ins. Beautiful great room has wall of built-ins, bank of windows, hardwood floors & wet bar. Formal dining room features bay window w/ French doors opening up to a lovely sunroom w/Mexican tile & windows overlooking the backyard. Four lg bedrooms (2 master suites, one w/fireplace) & 3 full baths on 2nd floor. Unfinished attic space waiting for personal touch. Deck offers great space for entertaining in serene setting. Recent updates include: roof '02, furnace '07, garage door & Genie '09, updated electric & box '97, & both master baths. Hardwood floors throughout! Walking distance to public schools! Enjoy leisurely walks to Historic Downtown Hudson!

Presented By:

11/12/2010

Bobi Schultz

Primary: 330-562-6188
Secondary: 330-998-3490
Other:
E-mail: bobischultz@howardhanna.com
Web Page: http://bobischultz.howardhanna.com

Howard Hanna

195 Barrington Town Square Dr.
Aurora, OH 44202
330-562-6188
Fax: 330-562-6352
See our listings online:
http://www.howardhanna.com

Featured properties may not be listed by the office/agent presenting this brochure.

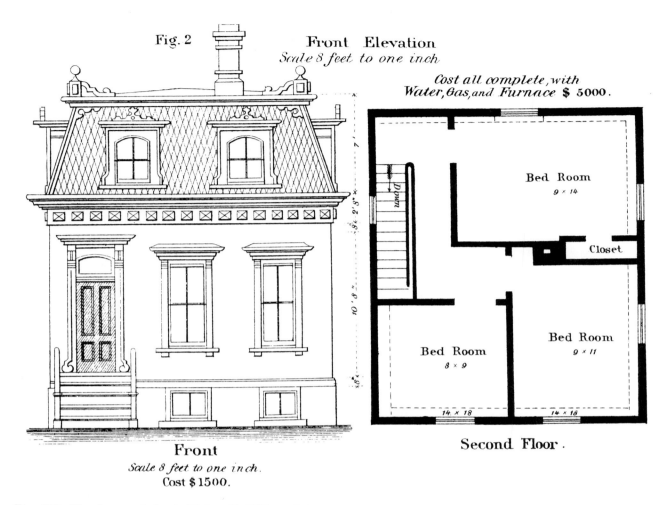

Fig. 2   Front Elevation
Scale 8 feet to one inch

Cost all complete, with
Water, Gas, and Furnace $ 5000.

Bed Room
9 × 14

Down

Closet

Bed Room
8 × 9

Bed Room
9 × 11

14 × 18   14 × 18

Second Floor.

Front
Scale 8 feet to one inch.
Cost $1500.

Fig. 120. The cheapest design in Bicknell's Village Builder *of 1873 was this tiny mansard-roofed cottage.*

Fig. 121. The Ichabod Compton, Jr., house has enjoyed two high-style architectural lives, first as a Federal house, then remodeled in the Second Empire fashion. (Cumberland County Department of Planning and Development, under contract with Robert Watson)

Fig. 122. In 1877 the ashlar brownstone used to build the David Stout house was a traditional material used for a modern style.

Fig. 123. A concave roof with convex towers highlights the three-dimensional quality of the best Second Empire houses.

Fig. 124. (opposite) Isaac Hobbs and his son were Philadelphia architects who designed most of the house plans published monthly in Godey's Lady's Book. *In 1871 they collected their most popular designs in book form, the source of this illustration. (Avery Architectural and Fine Arts Library, Columbia University in the City of New York)*

DESIGN XXIX.

A Model Residence.

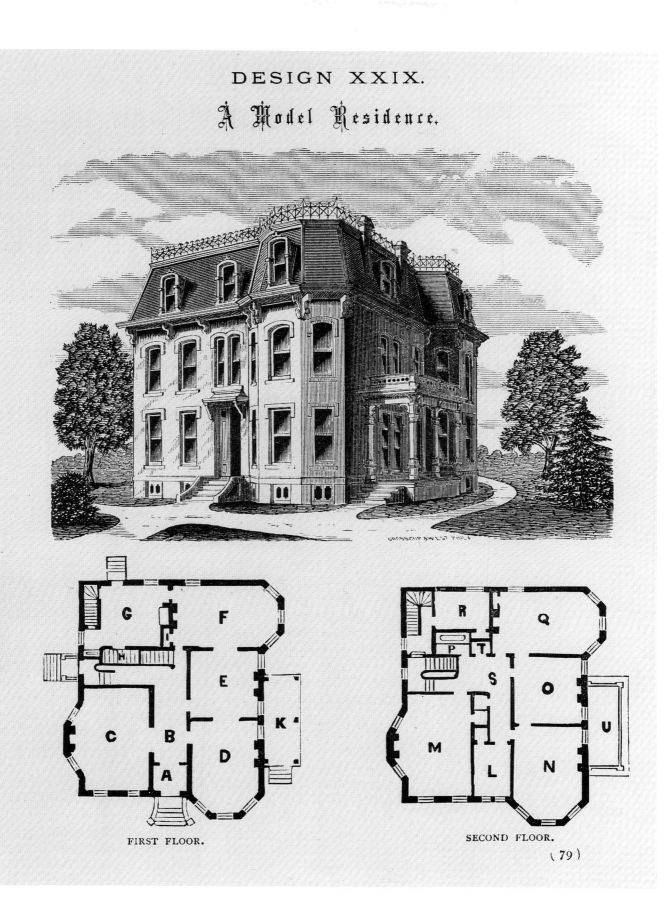

FIRST FLOOR.

SECOND FLOOR.

(79)

Fig. 125. *Advertisement for a toilet from* How to Build, Furnish, and Decorate, *1883.*

Fig. 126. *Advertisement for a cooking stove from* Scientific American Architect and Builders Edition, *1887.*

Domestic Mechanicals

In 1857, when Calvert Vaux wrote *Villas and Cottages*, it seemed perfectly reasonable, even progressive, for him to describe a "simple suburban cottage" where the kitchen sink was set on the back porch. At least there *was* a kitchen sink. In describing the same cottage, he noted that "the chamber plan shows three bedrooms and a large linen closet with a window in it. This, if preferred, could be used as a bathroom."

By the time the Second Empire style had reached its zenith, American domestic comfort was well served by technological achievements of substantial sophistication, but the era's pattern books still had to argue for certain basic improvements. As late as 1887 the author of *Shoppell's Modern Houses* felt it informative to pose the question, "Shall we have plumbing in the house, or shall we not?" Shoppell's answer was, "You can have the plumbing without danger to health, at a small original outlay, and with no repair bills, if it is designed and put in properly in the first place, and at the time the house is built. To put plumbing in an old house that was not designed to receive it is very expensive and troublesome work."

In the same article, "About Plumbing," Shoppell struck a moderately pro-feminist stance by insisting "that the great saving of woman's strength and patience when the house is provided with running water, stationary wash-tubs, bath, etc., is only appreciated by those who have had the care of a house not provided with them." By the last quarter of the nineteenth century pattern books often included advertisements for these and other labor-saving home appliances. A surprising choice of sanitary ware was available (Fig. 125); innovative cooking ranges with a variety of fuel options had reached a large market (Fig. 126); and home heating could be achieved with a central furnace or improved stoves (Fig. 127).

No pattern-book author had succeeded, however, in imagining how these machines might change the function and appearance of the house itself. No author envisaged an integrated system wrought from a combination of all these separate mechanicals, a system that addressed the real needs for efficiency and freedom from drudgery of the domestic manager, the woman of the house. No author but one. In 1869 Catherine Beecher, sister of Harriet Beecher Stowe, published *American Woman's Home*. For her experimental house (Fig. 128) she created an open floor plan the likes of which had never been seen, with specialized built-in furniture and labor-saving equipment. James Marston Fitch has called Catherine Beecher's house "a true machine for living," filled with features of "astonishing modernity." In *Architecture and the Aesthetics of Plenty* Fitch lauds Beecher's "services [as] quite complex and highly developed. She links a basement hot-air furnace, Franklin stoves, and a kitchen range into a central heating and ventilating system of some sophistication. She has eliminated all fireplaces as dirty and inefficient. The house is now served with an essentially modern plumbing system."

Beecher's scheme, unprecedented in its combination of technological and social implications, made the outlook of her male contemporaries seem timid and fragmented. Among pattern-book authors it was only Orson Squire Fowler who came close to matching her vision. Apart from Beecher's own house, we search in vain in New Jersey or anywhere else for built examples of this American woman's home. So radical were her ideas that they had to wait half a century before they were implemented in anything like the way she had intended.

Fig. 127. Advertisement for a furnace from How to Build, Furnish, and Decorate, 1883.

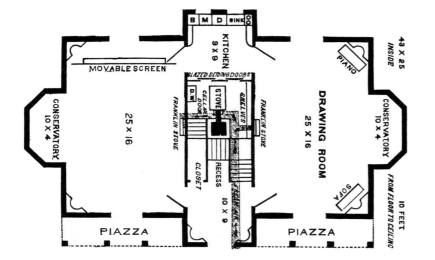

Fig. 128. The plan from Catherine Beecher's American Woman's Home, published in 1869, featured large airy rooms, a kitchen with built-in cupboards, and a portable screen in the main room for privacy.

137

4

ECLECTICISM PREVAILS

The year was 1886, and the *Scientific American Architects and Builders Edition* was impressed with New Jersey's suburban growth:

> The open countryside adjacent to the city of New York is in many respects most beautiful and attractive. This is especially the case in respect to the region situated westerly from the metropolis. . . . The scenery in all directions is interesting, and here are scattered hundreds of hamlets, villages, and rural cities, where thousands of people, doing business in the great city, have built their dwellings. We have thought our readers might be interested in knowing something concerning the houses and their surroundings; for this purpose we have selected, as a type, the suburban town of Passaic City, N.J.[1]

Depicted in the article's first illustration (Fig. 129) were carriages passing on a tree-shaded avenue, a well-dressed couple boating in bucolic surroundings, and, most telling, a train bringing

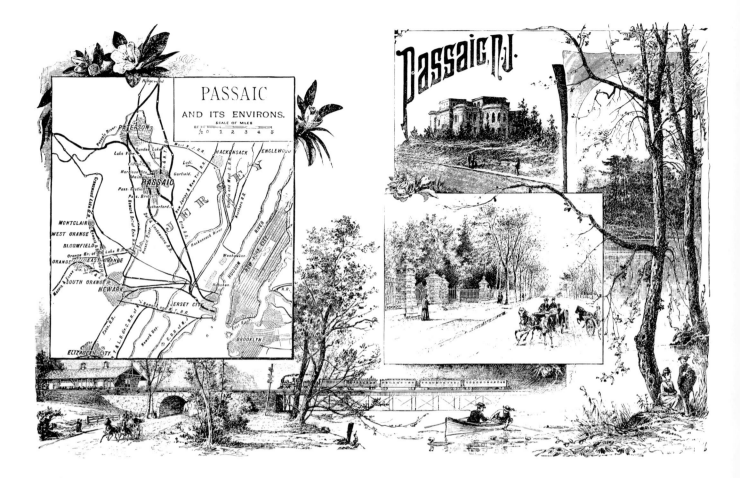

Fig. 129. Verdant, semi-rural surroundings were almost as important to the promoters of New Jersey suburbs as tasteful and convenient dwellings, a fact made abundantly clear by this illustration from the Scientific American Architects and Builders Edition.

commuters home to a neat, Stick Style depot. More and better railroad lines were one important reason that residential construction reached a furious pace in New Jersey suburbs between 1875 and 1900, a period marked by explosive growth not only for the building trades but for the architectural-book publishing business as well.

As travel between towns, and between New Jersey and New York, became ever easier, the railroads themselves engaged in land speculation. The Central Railroad of New Jersey created a subsidiary corporation, the Central New Jersey Land Improvement Company, expressly for building towns like Dunellen along its right of way. When not building new towns, the railroads were busy promoting existing ones. A pocket-size book titled *The Central Railroad of New Jersey*, published in 1890, was filled with boosterism like this paean to Plainfield:

The streets run in broad avenues, shaded by superb trees, with lines of fine residences and ample, well-kept grounds on either side. Closely trimmed lawns, flower beds and shrubs vary the level expanse. This part of the city seems to have been developed as a whole, and with the one purpose of making it unsurpassed for spaciousness and beauty.[2]

Brimming with pattern-book houses, these suburban towns were desirable for many reasons. According to the *New York Herald* of April 19, 1877:

New York is gradually, year by year, becoming the home of the very rich and the very poor. The middle classes are surely, rapidly, and permanently removing to the neighboring localities; the ample railroad facilities to all places embracing a radius of twenty miles around the city, together with cheap rents, pure air, and freedom from infectious diseases caused by dirty streets and other causes prevailing in large cities, tending to make residences in such places more and more sought for every year by old New York residents.[3]

Population growth from natural increase as well as migration fueled the building boom. The population of Orange grew from 4,385 in 1850 to 9,343 in 1870; in Plainfield the 1860 population of 3,224 had increased to 13,000 by 1890. Similar statistics pertained throughout northern and central New Jersey. "There is now building everywhere," reported *The Jerseyman* in 1887, and so it seemed.

The combination of better building and printing technologies, improved travel, and a growing population was more than sufficient reason for a new boom in pattern-book houses. Of the 658 practical architectural books published in America before 1895, two-thirds appeared between 1866 and 1894.[4] As the building boom gained momentum, however, the picturesque architectural modes of the first half of the nineteenth century did not disappear overnight. The Gothic, especially, assumed new guises and entered the vernacular mainstream in greatly changed ways. This impulse toward novelty and picturesque expression produced an architecture of larger scale and greater complexity than that of the years before the Civil War.

A Decade of Confusion

The 1870s were a decade of fumblings and false starts for American architecture. Something new was wanted, but architects and the public alike were uncertain what form it should take. The Second Empire style was on the decline, while Carpenters'

Gothic and cross-gabled "almost Italianate" farmhouses proliferated (Fig. 130), dressed with the jigsawn ornament that is the emblem of Victorian-era building (Fig. 131). Books like *Woodward's National Architect*, published in 1869, included designs for houses that defy easy stylistic labels. Some were derived from the Gothic cottage, some were called Swiss (Fig. 132), while others were clearly what has since been named the Stick Style. Their commonality is found in flat, sawn, and incised ornamental members that express angularity instead of the curvilinear and carved qualities of the Gothic and Italianate houses that were Downing's legacy.

Fig. 130. The center-gabled house adorned with a dripping, jigsawn bargeboard become a familiar feature of the New Jersey townscape during the 1860s and on into the 1870s, even as more complex styles competed for the public's attention.

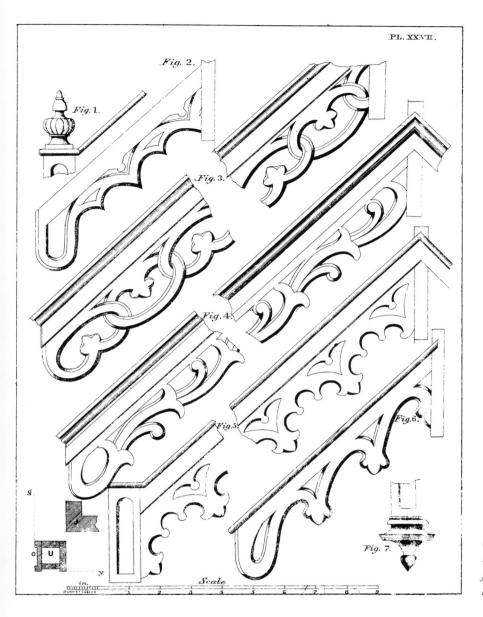

Fig. 131. Oliver Smith's The Domestic Architect *(1845) was one of many sources for decorated bargeboard designs popular during the middle of the nineteenth century.*

Houses in these angular modes gained some measure of popularity thanks to the work of several architects and pattern-book authors.

Although better known today for his Italianate designs, Samuel Sloan also tried his hand at the new, angular style. Three of his designs were published in an 1875 book by Amos Jackson Bicknell called *Bicknell's Wooden and Brick Buildings with Details.* Sloan must have fashioned these designs a few years before the book went to press, because two of them, bearing Bicknell's numbers 17 and 18, were built in Haddonfield in 1874. They stood just west of the Camden and Amboy Railroad on a tract of farmland that had been

Engr'd & print by KORFF BROTHERS 54 William St. N.

Fig. 132. Crisp horizontal, vertical, and diagonal lines characterize this "Swiss" cottage published in Woodward's National Architect *in 1869.*

assembled by the Haddonfield Land and Improvement Company, another example of speculative development tied to railroad ambitions. In 1871 several lots in the tract were bought by William Massey "of Philadelphia," explanation enough for the work of a Philadelphia architect being found in New Jersey.[5] The nature of Massey's business connection with Sloan is unclear, but the speculative intent of his building venture is evident from an 1874 newspaper notice:

> We had the privilege lately of inspecting one of the elegant houses put up by Mr. Massey, and were much pleased with it. It appears to be well built, with the best materials, and furnished throughout with gas and water pipes. The rooms are well supplied with windows and are light and airy. It has about half an acre of ground; it is situated on Washington Avenue, near the railroad depot, and it is altogether a very convenient, pleasant and desirable property.[6]

An analysis of this brief note tells us several things about the houses Sloan was designing and the state of domestic architecture in the decade after the Civil War. Piped gas and water "throughout" were still sufficiently notable to merit mention. Plentiful light and air, domestic prerequisites for the health-conscious mid-Victorians, were made possible by the manufacture of cheaper plate glass in larger sizes. The building lot of "about half an acre" was designed to maximize Mr. Massey's profit margin, a far cry from the genuine villa sites with generous landscaping potential discussed by A. J. Downing thirty years earlier. Finally, a location "near the railroad depot" was the essential fact that made all of this subdivision and construction appealing to potential homeowners and gave the "railroad suburbs" their name.

An examination of Sloan's Design No. 18 (Fig. 133) shows why this mode of architecture was later christened the Stick Style. The entire surface of the house was divided into horizontal or vertical bands by clapboards, belt courses, and vertical cornerboards. Even the windows were set up in tight frames defined by these elements. Instead of relying for dramatic effect on bracketed eaves in the Italianate manner, Sloan pulled the steep gables forward into deep

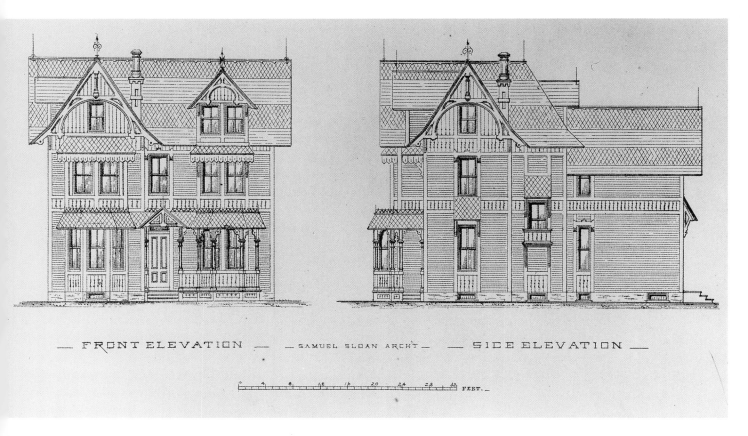

— FRONT ELEVATION — — SAMUEL SLOAN ARCH'T — — SIDE ELEVATION —

FEET.

Fig. 133. A world removed from his volumetric masonry designs in the Italianate style, this Stick Style house by Samuel Sloan suggests the light balloon frame beneath its taut wooden "skin."

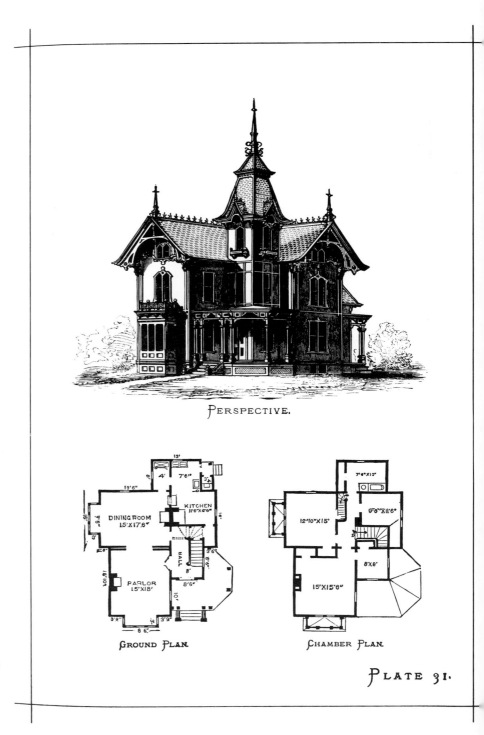

PERSPECTIVE.

GROUND PLAN.

DINING ROOM
15'X17'6"

KITCHEN
11'6"X6'6"

HALL
8'

PARLOR
15'X18'

CHAMBER PLAN.

12'10"X15'

9'8"X11'6"

8'X8'

15'X15'6"

PLATE 31.

Fig. 134. Published in 1876 by E. C. Hussey, this house should look familiar. Though dressed up with stickwork and elaborated king posts in the gables, it is essentially Downing's towered villa of 1842.

projections finished with flat-sawn bargeboards and decorated with king posts.

Similar sticklike elements were found in an 1875 design in E. C. Hussey's *Home Building* (Fig. 134). Although Hussey did not divide his wall surfaces into as many separate zones, he too relied on belt courses, cornerboards, prominent window frames, flat barge-boards, and gable king posts. A house from this design was built in the town of Wallingford for W. S. Anderson, whose "well-known lumber yards," according to Hussey, held "an extensive stock of all materials required in building houses."[7]

Although they had not abandoned traditional symmetry entirely, both Hussey and Sloan published plans that displayed a strong asymmetrical bent. Combined with crisp angularity and complex but flat surface ornament, this movement toward asymmetry marked an important transition in domestic architectural style and its presentation in pattern books. Balloon framing had made it easier for architects to imagine all of these changes.

Queen Anne Reigns

The architect and author whose work best describes the evolution of pattern-book taste during this transitional period is Henry Hudson Holly (1834–1892), whose first book, *Holly's Country Seats*, was published in New York City in 1863. His designs are bedded securely in the Bracketed-Italianate-Gothic modes promoted by Downing, but also presage the angularity of the 1870s. The lithographs in *Country Seats* are soft-edged and atmospheric, subtle reflections of their Romantic character. Many of the designs are for mansions, but Holly noted that one small T-plan cottage, Design No. 1, "was built for John W. Shedden, Esq., on the Morris and Essex Railroad, about one mile beyond South Orange, N.J." Design No. 15 in the same book included an unusual rustic summer house with a viewing platform (Fig. 135). An old photograph shows that the same summer house was built in a private garden in Llewllyn Park (Fig. 136).

In 1878 Holly brought out *Modern Dwellings in Town and Country*. Here he pledged his allegiance to the "free classic" or Queen Anne style, which had just been introduced to the United States by the British Government buildings at the Centennial Exposition in Philadelphia. In *Modern Dwellings*, Holly admired the work of contemporary English architects and proposed nothing less than the creation of a new American vernacular building style based on a combination of high-style Elizabethan and Jacobean buildings and English cottages, which, he observed, "are partly timbered, partly covered with tile hangings, and have tall and spacious chimneys of considerable merit."[8] If we substite American wooden shingles for English tile hangings, we find that Holly had isolated three important elements of what would grow into the American Queen Anne style (Fig. 137).

In *Modern Dwellings*, Holly presented his designs in crisp line drawings, the better to convey the essential contrast between dif-

Fig. 135. Henry Hudson Holly thought enough of this design for a summer house to repeat it on the cover of his first book, Holly's Country Seats.

Fig. 136: Rustic-work gazebos, bridges, and fences ornamented the communal grounds of Llewellyn Park, one of the first planned suburbs in the United States, where this summer house was built in a private garden.

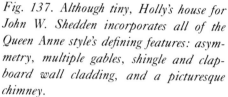

Fig. 137. Although tiny, Holly's house for John W. Shedden incorporates all of the Queen Anne style's defining features: asymmetry, multiple gables, shingle and clapboard wall cladding, and a picturesque chimney.

ferent materials—clapboard, shingle, brick, slate—and the decorative details that animated the style. Their large size, complex massing, and reliance on fine finishes and details all reflected the fact that they were houses intended for people of means; so too did Holly's frequent references to the era's foremost decorators and furniture manufacturers in his extensive section devoted to interior decoration. The complex massing and varied surface treatments typical of the style were repeated throughout the book, but the best surviving example of Holly's work is found in a house he designed shortly after publication of *Modern Dwellings*. Exhibiting the same Queen Anne characteristics splashed so freely across the pages of his pattern book, this is a house in Llewellyn Park created for the department store executive Henry C. Pedder (Fig. 138).

Later famous as "Glenmont," the home of Thomas Edison, this extravagant and rather English-looking house was published in the August 27, 1881 issue of *American Architect and Building News* (Fig. 139). Its towering, paneled chimneys, brick, clapboard, shingle, and half-timbered walls, steep roofs, repeated gables, and asymmetrical massing are elements that continued to define the Queen Anne style as it descended from the hands of architects into the pattern-book mainstream. In addition to varied details and exaggerated asymmetry, Queen Anne houses relied on condensed details used as design focal points. This practice is illustrated by the frontispiece to *Modern Dwellings*. The gabled entry it depicts

(Fig. 140) resembles the entry to a house called "The Kedge," in Morristown (Fig. 141), which had been enlarged in the new style in the 1880s.

Like Downing, Holly meant to educate public taste. In its fifty chapters, *Modern Dwellings* ranged from considerations of siting and building materials, heating and ventilating, to chapters titled "Durability and Honesty in Furniture" and "Ladies as Wall Decorators." Although such coverage was encyclopedic, it was not aimed at the general house-building public. Aesthetically persuasive as the small drawings in *Modern Dwellings* were, Holly's elite readers would not have been foolish enough to try and build from them. So although Holly was enormously influential in cultivating a taste for the Queen Anne in affluent quarters, the style gained genuinely widespread popularity in other ways, principally by mail.

The New York architectural firm of Cleveland and Backus had developed the idea of house plans by mail as early as 1856,

Fig. 138. The several additions absorbed by Glenmont have made it even more archetypically Queen Anne than it was when first published in 1881.

Fig. 139. Glenmont's half-timbering and tall paneled chimneys are clues to the architect's infatuation with English models.

and even Holly offered them on a limited basis. However, it was George and Charles Palliser who first brought the Queen Anne style to a mass audience through pattern books supported by mail-order plans.[9] Working for a time as carpenter-developers, producing block after block of houses, the brothers began to wonder if a market might exist for more individualized houses at mass-built prices. In 1876, drawing on their considerable practical experience, they published a pamphlet-size pattern book titled *Model Homes for the People, A Complete Guide to the Proper and Economical Erection of Buildings*. Almost immediately they sold more than five thousand copies. Not only had they identified a need, they had found a way to satisfy it cheaply. *Model Homes* sold for twenty-five cents at a time when most larger pattern books cost between three and ten dollars. Over the next thirty years Palliser, Palliser and Company published at least twenty pattern books. Moving beyond their original, pamphlet-size success, they employed a large-page format that enabled them to combine plans and elevations with large-scale details (Fig. 142).

Their most significant innovation, however, was their mail-order service. After selecting a house design, the pattern-book

Fig. 140. Above the porch roof in this engraving from Holly's Modern Dwellings *is a panel-with-garland, reminding us that another name for Queen Anne architecture was "free classic."*

reader completed a questionnaire about such matters as lot size, house orientation, and budget. Upon returning this to the Pallisers with a fee considerably less than that charged by architects, the customer received complete working drawings for a house "customized" from the pattern-book design. That the system worked, and that it worked in New Jersey, is proven by a contract dated

Fig. 141. The designer of The Kedge is unknown, although family tradition credits Stanford White with remodeling the house. The similarity between its entry and the one depicted by Holly emphasizes the vocabulary common to Queen Anne architecture of the 1880s.

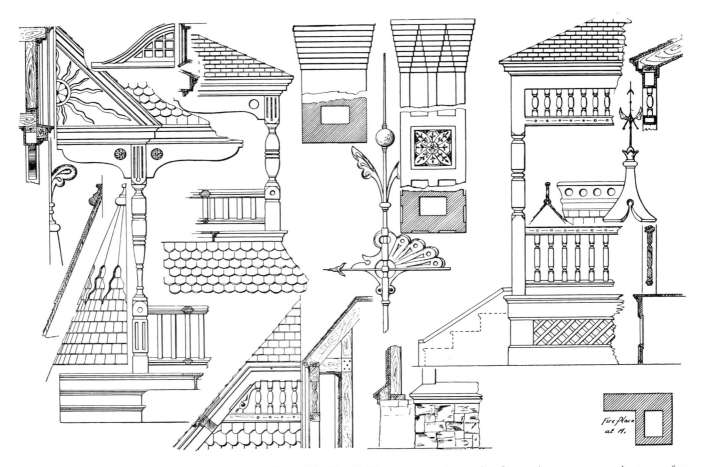

Fig. 142. The Pallisers presented complex Queen Anne ornament in page after page of drawings sufficiently detailed to show carpenters precisely what they intended. This page comes from their 1887 book, New Cottage Homes and Details.

April 16, 1883 between J. D. Brown, contractor, and Mary Burgess of the village of Highlands. The contract specified that "on or before the first day of July," J. D. Brown will furnish the "whole of the carpenter's work required in the erection and completion of a new Frame Dwelling house & Barn building . . . to the Plans, Drawings and Specifications prepared for the said work by Palliser, Palliser & Co." The contract was cosigned by Charles and George Palliser.[10]

The Pallisers' success was due in large part to their abandoning the theorizing and philosophy of earlier pattern-book writers in favor of practical information drawn from their own construction experience. So conscious were they of mass-marketing opportunities that they continued to publish designs for cheaper houses even after the success of their large-format books. During the 1890s the

Red Bank Register was one of several newspapers that featured a regular column of Palliser plans and perspective drawings. One, titled "A Sensible House" (Fig. 143), appeared in the July 7, 1897 issue. It depicted a comfortable eight-room house that illustrated the Queen Anne style at its most modest, stripped of ornament but retaining its dominant gables, bays, veranda, and asymmetrical massing. Designs like this were a mirror of the style at the end of its popularity in New Jersey.

Robert W. Shoppell and his Co-operative Building Plan Association were worthy competitors who emulated the Pallisers in every way. Shoppell, too, offered working drawings and detailed specifications by mail. He produced numerous titles, beginning in 1881 with *Artistic Modern Houses of Low Cost*. Although varied in their stylistic choices, Shoppell's books and serial publications favored the Queen Anne style. Despite this enthusiasm, Shoppell himself was wary of fashionable terminology: "In this work," he wrote in 1886, "we decided not to use the term 'Queen Anne' or any other fancy titles for our homes. If 'Queen Anne' means beauty and novelty of design (which seems to be the popular definition rather than having reference to an old English style), most of our designs might be called 'Queen Anne.'"[11]

The dense details and large houses published by the Pallisers in their more costly books of the 1880s helped to popularize the taste for Queen Anne elaboration, but they were really only one step removed from the very expensive architect-designed Queen Anne houses favored by Holly. Shoppell, by contrast, was in dead earnest when he dedicated the Co-operative Building Plan Association to low-cost architectural services:

Before this business was established it was very difficult, if not impossible, to get full architectural services for a price that the public considered low and reasonable. The architect who makes the drawings and specifications for one client only cannot do the work on a small house, say a $1,500 house, for less than $100. . . . While these fees were not unfair, but, in fact, were well worth their cost, it is indisputable that the public found them too high, and the consequence was that most of the houses of moderate cost were built from *carpenter's* designs, and lacked the beauty and unity, convenience and economy of arrangement that comes from the employment of architects. Our fees, at less than one quarter the regular rates, effectually met the necessities of the situation.[12]

Shoppell was well aware of the ill feeling that his particular brand of architectural services might engender, however. He was clearly on the defensive when he wrote:

A SENSIBLE HOUSE.

A Design Which Combines Beauty and Utility.

[Copyright, 1897, by George Palliser, 32 Park place, New York.]

The handling of property contiguous to large cities has become quite a science in the past few years, and much hard and earnest work has been done in the line of the development of rough grounds to a state of home building uses, and it has frequently happened that those who had the least financially at the start have made the most out of the transactions. The rich man is generally a very poor real estate agent, with no time to push or boom his property and place it on the market. For this reason many bad failures have oc-

PERSPECTIVE VIEW.

Fig. 143. By the end of the 1890s the richly overloaded detailing of the Queen Anne style had all but disappeared. This crudely drawn Palliser design meant for newspaper publication was aimed at a middle-class market.

Many reputable architects do not approve of our business, for the simple reason that we have cut the regular rates of charges. These gentlemen should remember that our patronage comes largely from those who would not employ architects, except at low charges. . . . We do not believe there is a single influence today that benefits the architectural profession so much as the wide dissemination of our plans and books.[13]

Shoppell's promotional language may sound boastful, but the evidence suggests that his claims mirrored reality. More than one carpenter, for example, took pains to establish a Shoppell connection: "Warren C. Conklin, Contractor and Builder. Experienced and Trustworthy. Guarantees strict attention and satisfaction. I make a specialty of figuring on plans of *Shoppell's Modern Houses*. Prepared to do work in any part of state. Residence, Oceanic, New Jersey."[14]

Testimonials from across the country prove that the services of the Co-operative Building Plan Association were used in precisely the manner Shoppell described. In 1894 he published letters that included sixteen from satisfied New Jersey clients. Among the towns represented were Bridgeton, Butler, Irvington, Jamesburg, Little Falls, New Brunswick, Paterson, Rahway and Sparta. A letter from Madison was typical:

I will say that I regard the Co-operative Building Plan Association superior to ordinary architects. The plans drawn for me were correct in all measurements. My carpenter tells me that the timbers cut by your measurements always come out right. My house, built by your plans, both inside and out, has been greatly admired, and has been pronounced the prettiest in our town. . . . When I build again, if I ever do, the Co-operative Building Plan Association will be my architect.

Respectfully yours,
EDWARD MILLER[15]

Building a Pattern-Book Neighborhood

Edward Miller's "greatly admired" new house was a symbol of his material success; only five years earlier he had opened a butcher shop on Main Street in Madison, which "quickly won for him many friends."[16] The neighborhood where he built his pattern-book house was just opening up; between 1885 and the end of the century it grew into a neat middle-class enclave. Evidence of the local building boom was a notice in the June 4, 1886 issue of *The Jerseyman*: "Smith Bros., Lumber Dealers, who purchased of Mrs. Alfred Brittin not long since her lot on Railroad Avenue, are cutting a road through this property, which is to run parallel to Green Avenue. This road has been named Maple Street." Only a month later the paper informed its readers that "a large number of lots have been sold by Smith and Co., on their new street."

A plate from Robinson's Atlas of 1887 (Fig. 144) made the speculative basis of the new street and its subsequent development easy to understand. The vacant lots laid out by the Smith Brothers were evident. Their Sash & Blind Factory could be seen on property that backed up to Maple Avenue, and just beyond the railroad tracks lay the lumberyard of E. L. Cook. According to the *Madison Eagle* of October 19, 1888, "E. L. Cook is building two tasty houses on Maple Avenue after having sold a portion of his late purchase of land to Fred A. Miller, F. I. Hannon and J. D. Burnet. The last named will build at once. Mr. Cook has also bought another block of five lots for improvement." No better formula could exist for the success of small-town capitalists: the subdividers and developers of this tract were the purveyors of the plumbing, sash, blinds, lumber, and millwork necessary to build the houses erected upon it.

Throughout the 1880s and 1890s and on into the teens of the twentieth century, *The Madison Eagle* reported additional subdivisions, property transfers, new construction, and numerous rentals on Maple, Green, and adjoining Prospect Street, where the names Smith, Cook, and James D. Burnet, carpenter, were a measure of the neighborhood's growth. The Madison directories for the same years provided a good idea of who moved into these new houses, sometimes, it seems, before the paint had had time to dry. There were two butchers (the Miller brothers), several carpenters (including James D. Burnet himself), a music teacher and a bookkeeper, a plumber, an electrical engineer, a tinsmith, two basket makers, clerks, cashiers, a surveyor, and an undertaker, among others. A few worked in Manhattan (the Delaware, Lackawanna and Western station stood two blocks distant), but for the most part these were people who furnished local goods and services. Their economic and social standing proved Robert Shoppell's claim that "this is the only architectural publication that we know of that is issued in the interest of the people." The people in question must have agreed, because many of the neighborhood's new houses (and the majority of those on Maple Avenue) were built from Shoppell's designs.

Edward Miller's house (Fig. 145) set the architectural style for new construction in the neighborhood. Its large cross-gables, shin-

Fig. 144. An 1887 plate from Robinson's Atlas of Morris County shows Maple Avenue filling up with what we know from other sources to be pattern-book houses.

gled and half-timbered attic story, and porch adorned with flat fan brackets are typical of Shoppell's vocabulary.

Number 45 Maple Avenue (Fig. 146), built from Shoppell's Design Number 203 (Fig. 147), repeats the same cross-gabled shape and the indispensable Queen Anne combination of clapboard and shingle cladding. Even the windows made by the Smith Brothers sash and blind factory followed the published design.

The most picturesque house in the neighborhood is 33 Maple Avenue (Fig. 148). It is also one of the least altered houses on the street, with all of the details intact that appear in Shoppell's Design Number 172 (Fig. 149), published in March 1886. C. M. Bush was one of the first to purchase a lot on Maple Avenue, buying from Edward Smith in May 1886. On October 22, 1886, *The Madison Eagle* reported that "C. M. Bush has moved into his new home on Maple Avenue." According to a subsequent article in the same newspaper, Cornelius and his new bride named their house "Cosey Cottage."

The Madison Eagle and *The Jerseyman* chronicled the fortunes of the Maple and Green avenues neighborhood assiduously. From 1886 to 1889 the papers ran almost weekly accounts of property sales, construction news, and announcements of families taking possession of their new homes (Fig. 150). Sidewalks, sewers, and other public improvements were newsworthy events during the same years.

Some of the neighborhood houses that cannot be matched precisely to Shoppell's books were undoubtedly built from Cooperative Building Plan Association designs, since their decorative motifs and plans are so similar to the firm's work. The published designs often bore notes like "this design can be reversed, en-

Fig. 145. Edward Miller's house in Madison is typical of the neighborhood's small Queen Anne dwellings built from designs published by the Co-operative Building Plan Association.

larged, reduced, or altered to suit special wants. The specifications can be altered also, to employ different materials that may be best or cheapest in any locality." [17] The Maple Avenue houses display just such reversals or substitutions, some of them probably reflective of the trim and millwork that Smith and E. L. Cook were selling around the corner.

One consistent difference between the designs presented by Shoppell and the way they were built in Madison is their siting. The published perspective drawings (see Fig. 147, for example) depicted houses in spacious landscape settings, without neighbors in sight. The reality that made such houses affordable to Madison's

Fig. 146. The builder of this Maple Avenue house reproduced the interior and exterior of Shoppell's design exactly.

plumbers and butchers demanded building lots with frontage that rarely exceeded fifty feet. Although the popular press called these parcels "villa lots," the conditions they expressed were far denser than the rural-suburban ideal of A. J. Downing and Henry Hudson Holly.

Like the lots they occupied, the Shoppell houses on Maple Avenue were small, often measuring no more than twenty-one by thirty-six feet, notably smaller than the Queen Anne mansions

Fig. 147. (opposite) Published in Shoppell's Modern Houses *in 1889, this is the source for 45 Maple Avenue. (Art and Architecture Collection, Miriam and Ira D. Wallach Division of Art, Prints, and Photographs, The New York Public Library, Astor, Lenox, and Tilden Foundations)*

DESIGN No. 203. PERSPECTIVE VIEW

DESCRIPTION OF DESIGN NUMBER 203

SIZE OF STRUCTURE: Front, 24 ft., 6 in. Side, 35 ft., inclusive of veranda.

SIZE OF ROOMS: See floor plans.

HEIGHT OF STORIES: Cellar, 6 ft., 6 in.; First Story, 9 ft.; Second Story, 8 ft., 3 in.; Third Story, open attic.

MATERIALS: Foundation, stone; First Story, clapboards; Second Story, shingles; Gables, paneled; Roof, shingled.

COST: $1,800, all complete, except grates or heaters.

[*See the first pages of this book for information about details, specifications, bill of quantities and working plans of this design.*]

NOTES

The cost is figured from prices of material and labor in the neighborhood of New York City, October, 1885. In most other localities the cost is less —in some places much less. A different date also modifies cost. The publishers will be glad to acquaint the intending builder with this modified cost at any time.

FIRST FLOOR. NO. 203

SPECIAL FEATURES.—A cellar under the whole house, with access to it from the kitchen. A stairway to the attic is provided, where two good rooms can be finished if desired.

Wide openings between the hall, parlor and dining-room make these apartments very attractive and roomy. The central and corner windows of the dining-room give a beautiful bay-window effect to that apartment.

In the second story are four bed-rooms and a bath-room, each with a good closet.

A good way to heat this house is by fireplace heaters in the parlor and dining-room, which would heat the two chambers above also. The hall and other bed-rooms, except in the coldest weather, would receive sufficient heat from the other rooms to be comfortable.

A furnace in the cellar would heat the house more perfectly, and we will indicate the proper position of the pipes and registers on the plans if it is desired to use one.

To enlarge the accommodations of this house, a one-story kitchen extension can be built in the rear, at small expense; then, by removing the closet and pantry and the partition forming the present small rear hall, a fine sitting-room or library is obtained, which should be connected with the dining-room by a wide opening or double doors.

SECOND FLOOR. NO. 203

Fig. 148. Unlike so many Queen Anne "cottages" of heroic dimensions and multiple rooms, 33 Maple Avenue is appropriately diminutive. Its size inspired its name, "Cosey Cottage."

Fig. 149. (opposite) Shoppell's Design No. 172 and 33 Maple Avenue are mirror images. Even without palm trees, the built example is the most picturesque of the neighborhood's pattern-book houses. (Art and Architecture Collection, Miriam and Ira D. Wallach Division of Art, Prints, and Photographs, New York Public Library, Astor, Lenox, and Tilden Foundations)

DESIGN No. 172. PERSPECTIVE VIEW

DESCRIPTION OF DESIGN NUMBER 172

SIZE OF STRUCTURE: Front, 30 ft., including veranda. Side, 40 ft., including veranda and bay-window.

SIZE OF ROOMS: See floor plans.

HEIGHT OF STORIES: First Story, 10 ft.; Second Story, 9 ft.

MATERIALS: Foundation, wood posts set in concrete or brick piers; First Story, clapboards; Second story, shingles, Roof, shingles.

COST: $1,500, complete, except heater.

[See the first pages of this book for information about details, specifications, bill of quantities and working plans of these designs]

SPECIAL FEATURES.—With its broad veranda and open fireplaces this design is specially suitable for a Southern, Seaside or Summer Cottage. The kitchen is in a small detached building in the rear.

In fact, however, it is well adapted for any climate. A fireplace heater in the parlor or dining-room easily warms the three bed-rooms up stairs. If a detached kitchen is not wanted the library can be turned into a kitchen, or a small, inexpensive addition can be built in the rear for a kitchen.

A cellar under the dining-room with strong plank walls will cost $35 additional; under the whole house with brick walls, $150.

The Painter's Specifications call for the body of the first story to be painted light brown; shingles on sides treated with crude petroleum; the roof stained red; trimmings olive; but these colors can be modified or entirely changed to suit the taste of the owner.

In Southern and Western States where materials and labor are cheap this house can be built for a much lower figure.

DESCRIPTION OF DESIGN NUMBER 173

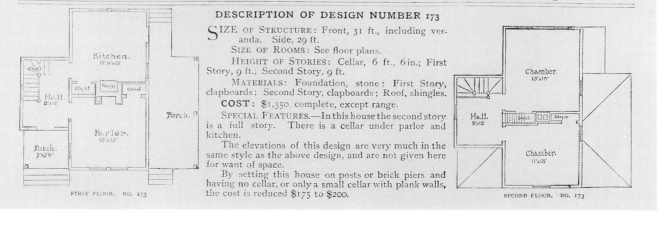

SIZE OF STRUCTURE: Front, 31 ft., including veranda. Side, 29 ft.

SIZE OF ROOMS: See floor plans.

HEIGHT OF STORIES: Cellar, 6 ft., 6 in.; First Story, 9 ft.; Second Story, 9 ft.

MATERIALS: Foundation, stone; First Story, clapboards; Second Story, clapboards; Roof, shingles.

COST: $1,350, complete, except range.

SPECIAL FEATURES.—In this house the second story is a full story. There is a cellar under parlor and kitchen.

The elevations of this design are very much in the same style as the above design, and are not given here for want of space.

By setting this house on posts or brick piers and having no cellar, or only a small cellar with plank walls, the cost is reduced $175 to $200.

FIRST FLOOR. NO. 173

SECOND FLOOR. NO. 173

inst., a dividend of three and one-half per cent. on the capital stock was declared from the earnings of the bank, payable on and after Jan. 2d, 1889.

W. F. MORROW,
Cashier.

THE undersigned has the pleasure to announce to the ladies in Madison and vicinity that he is prepared to make

ALL KINDS OF HAIR WORK,

such as frisettes, switches, etc., with which he may be favored.

H. STEADTRATH,
Over Dunning's tin store.

FIRST NATIONAL BANK.

MADISON, N. J., Dec. 13, 1888

THE annual meeting of stockholders for the election of directors of this bank for the ensuing year will be held at the banking house on Tuesday, the 8th day of January next, at ten o'clock A. M. Polls open from 10 to 11 A. M.

W. F. MORROW,
Cashier.

MRS. JAMES A. HENSEY,

(A GRADUATE OF THE HAGERSTOWN, MD., SEMINARY AND MUSICAL INSTITUTE,)

DESIRES TO SECURE PUPILS

ON

Either Piano or Organ.

Please address the above at Madison, New Jersey.

FOR RENT,

OR SALE.

A HOUSE JUST COMPLETED

on Maple Avenue,

Nine Rooms and Bath Room.

HEATING AND PLUMBING.

E. L. COOK.

2551.

Report of the Condition

OF THE

First National Bank of Madison,

at Madison, in the State of New Jersey, at the close of business, December 12, 1888.

RESOURCES.

Loans and discounts,	$137,497 32
U. S. Bonds to secure circulation,	12,500 00
Other stocks, bonds, and mortgages,	15,000 00
Due from approved reserve agents,	14,755 88
Due from other National Banks,	534 13
Real estate, furniture, and fixtures,	500 00
Current expenses and taxes paid,	1,449 80
Checks and other cash items,	434 80
Bills of other Banks,	530 00
Fractional paper currency, nickels and cents,	8 4½
Specie,	3,081 50
Legal tender notes,	4,733 00
Redemption fund with U. S. Treasurer [5 per cent. of circulation].	562 50
Total,	$191,587,40

LIABILITIES.

Capital stock paid in,	$50,000 00
Surplus fund,	11,500 00
Undivided profits,	[illegible]

WATCHES

Gold and Silver

FOR GENTS AND LADIES.

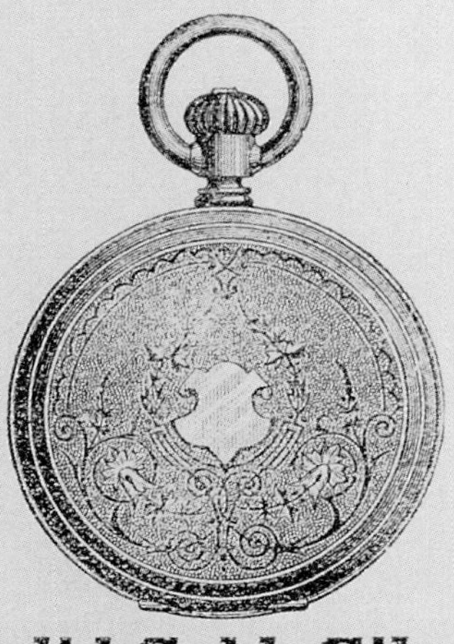

Solid Gold, Silver

AND PLATED JEWELRY.

Gold Pens, Pencils

Clocks and Silver Ware,

Spectacles and Eyeglasses,

at reduced prices for the holidays.

Repairing done in the best manner and warranted.

MAX REUTERSHAN,

Waverly Place, near Depot,

MADISON, N. J.

J. E. PARKER

The Jeweler,

of Morristown, N. J.,

Having sold out his interest in the SHOE BUSINESS, to John L. Bickford, Esq., of New York, will now give his whole TIME AND ATTENTION to the

Jewelry Business.

And shall be pleased to see all

Fig. 150. The social pages of The Madison Eagle *and advertisements such as this one, which appeared in December 1888, document the building of a pattern-book neighborhood.*

published by Holly and simpler than the villas published by the Pallisers. To serve its middle-class clients, the Co-operative Building Plan Association not only created smaller houses but simplified high-style Queen Anne features. Just as the Italianate and Gothic Revival styles of the 1850s and 1860s had evolved into their own vernacular carpenter's mode, so the Queen Anne style promoted by Henry Hudson Holly grew into the vernacular cottage he had predicted. In place of rambling, irregular plans, Shoppell's houses, the houses of the vernacular Queen Anne, *suggested* asymmetry by the addition of a few strategically placed bay windows and stairhall extensions to plans that were basically boxes. Even these affordable houses, however, displayed interiors that opened up space in a way new to American dwellings of modest cost. Thus the traditional side-hall and center-hall plans that had survived so many other stylistic innovations began finally to dissolve. As Shoppell wrote of his Design Number 192, "Throwing all of the rooms together by these wide openings practically makes one large apartment of the whole first floor, when desired. This gives an air of elegance and size to a small house that is astonishing."

Many of the small Maple Avenue houses could be built for $2,000 or less; Shoppell noted that the cost of Number 172, the Bushes' Cosey Cottage, was $1,500. Although Maple Avenue was remarkably homogeneous, the larger neighborhood enjoyed a degree of architectural and economic variety. E. L. Cook was building houses on adjacent Green Avenue as well, where some lots were a bit larger. On October 25, 1889, Judge George H. Yeaman and his family took possession of the house that Cook had just completed for them at 60 Green Avenue (Fig. 151). Built from the Co-operative Building Plan Association's Design Number 346 (Fig. 152), this more expensive house cost $4,500 and measured thirty-one by forty-six feet. One front corner was enlivened by a square tower over the entry, and the roof was clad in slate. Unlike some of Shoppell's designs, this one made a bathroom an integral part of the plan. Perhaps most useful for a family of the Yeamans' standing (he had been U.S. Minister to Denmark) were the seven bedrooms, which made plenty of space for servants' quarters.

One year earlier a house had been built from the same design at the other end of New Jersey, in Cape May, where it still stands. Shoppell designs were so popular that the deed for the Cape May house refers to the pattern-book plan by number.

Fig. 151. The house built for Judge George H. Yeaman and his family displays Shoppell's open tower glassed-in for winter. Several of the trim details differ from those depicted in the pattern-book design published three years earlier. (A Bill Redmond Photo)

Fig. 152. (opposite) The odd tower and almost mansardic roof make this one of Shoppell's more atypical Queen Anne designs.

DESIGN No. 346. PERSPECTIVE VIEW

DESCRIPTION OF DESIGN NUMBER 346

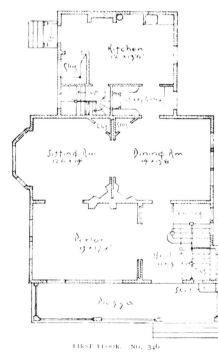

FIRST FLOOR. NO. 346

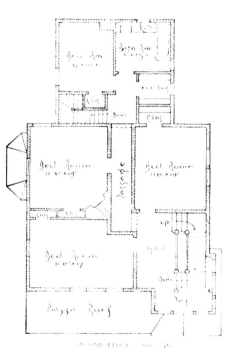

SECOND FLOOR. NO. 346

SIZE OF STRUCTURE: Front, 31 ft.; Side, 46 ft.

SIZE OF ROOMS: See floor plans.

HEIGHT OF STORIES: Cellar, 7 ft.; First Story, 10 ft.; Second Story, 9 ft.; Third Story, 8 ft.

MATERIALS: Foundation, stone and brick; First Story, clapboards; Second Story, shingles; Roof, slate.

COST: $4,500, complete, except mantels, kitchen range and heater.

[See page 147 for information about details, specifications, bill of quantities and working plans of this design.]

NOTES

The cost is figured from prices of material and labor in the neighborhood of New York City, June, 1886. In other localities and at different dates the cost will be somewhat modified. The publishers will be glad to acquaint the intending builder with this modified cost at any time.

This design can be reversed, enlarged, reduced or altered to suit special wants. The specifications can be altered, also, to employ different materials that may be best or cheapest in any locality.

SPECIAL FEATURES. Square hall, with platform staircase.

Sliding doors between hall and parlor and between sitting-room and dining-room.

Four bed-rooms, a bath-room, ample hall and large closets in the second story.

Three good bed-rooms in the third story.

Cellar under the whole house.

Eclectic Variations

Neighborhoods like the one in Madison were being built all over New Jersey during the 1880s and 1890s. Their moderate-size Queen Anne houses were affordable by almost anyone making more than a day laborer's wages. As the excerpts from Shoppell's publications prove, the pattern-book houses that filled these neighborhoods resulted from a new kind of relationship between architects and architectural publications. In order to make customized house plans available to a large number of buyers, pattern-book producers like the Co-operative Building Plan Association employed a staff of designers. Whether they were licensed or even trained architects is doubtful, but they were sufficiently skilled to produce convenient dwellings adorned with enough ornament to satisfy a buying public that was becoming more and more accustomed to consuming the products of an industrialized economy.

At the same time, the "high end" of the housing market was producing Queen Anne architecture of greater size and complexity, designed to satisy the more affluent arm of the conspicuously consuming public. Here, too, a new kind of relationship was being forged between architects and architectural publications. The earlier tradition of pattern books, which included the work of well-known architects (exemplified by Downing's publication of designs by A. J. Davis, John Notman, and Gervase Wheeler), continued on into the 1880s. A striking example of a Queen Anne house that fits this description is "The Anchorage" in Short Hills (Fig. 153). Although the work of a prominent firm, Lamb and Wheeler, the design was published in William T. Comstock's *Modern Architectural Designs and Details* in 1881 (Fig. 154). Part of Comstock's subtitle reads, "Comprising Original Drawings by a Number of Prominent Architects of Different Localities," a reminder that by this date a pattern book might still contain designs by a single architect-author or by a number of different architects. Its designs might be prepared expressly for the book in question or might illustrate houses already constructed. The Anchorage had probably been completed by the time Comstock's book saw print. Designed for one of New Jersey's more desirable new suburbs, it fell into the most typical, high-style Queen Anne mode of its day, characterized by pronounced asymmetry, multiple gables, and a mixture of materials. Its surviving ornament includes a prominent display of sunbursts and sunflowers, favorite motifs of the English Aesthetic Movement (Fig. 155). Houses like this were the epitome of what home builders came to think of as "Queen Anne." Comstock, however, advised in his preface that the entire school of dwellings sometimes called "Queen Anne," but also "Elizabethan, Jacobean, or Colonial," was "a revival of the old Gothic, as it appeared during the periods referred to under these respective names."

Although Comstock's book featured the work of successful architects, pattern books of the Queen Anne period were beginning to compete directly with the rising architectural profession. This was especially true of pattern books that promoted mail-order services like those of Palliser and Shoppell. *American Architect and Building News* had been founded as a professional journal in 1876, when the American version of the Queen Anne style was just gaining a foothold. By the 1880s it provided a platform from which its editors could rail against the debased designs of uneducated builders and pattern-book authors. Their antidote, of course, was the publication of architect-designed houses. In New Jersey, most of these were large suburban dwellings in prosperous towns like the Oranges, Montclair, Short Hills, and Englewood, or vacation cottages at Elberon and Monmouth Beach. Typical of the genre was a house designed by James Brown Lord for the new suburb of Short Hills Park. Published in the April 28, 1883 issue of *American Architect and Building News*, it was the kind of house meant for admiration and emulation (Fig. 156). *American Architect and Building News* was a pioneer in the publication of architectural photography. Lord's design appeared as a pen-and-ink drawing, probably because construction had not been completed by the publication date.

Architectural photographs in books and magazines enabled larger audiences to appreciate good architecture. One of the most opulent of the early photographic books was George William Sheldon's *Artistic Country Seats*, published in 1887. Sheldon featured many New Jersey houses, most now demolished. One that survives is a lavish Queen Anne house in North Plainfield (Fig. 157), designed by Charles H. Smith, who practiced in Manhattan and Plainfield. Smith's client in this case was Charles W. McCutchen, a partner in Holt and Company, export flour merchants in New York City, and a director of the Corn Exchange Bank. McCutchen was the kind of minor plutocrat Sheldon's book was meant to flatter, with a photograph (Fig. 158) that emphasized the solidity and massiveness of his new house. The photograph unintentionally documented the evolution of suburban taste in domestic architecture as well: to the left of the new house, just visible at the left edge of the frame, was the old McCutchen homestead, a board-and-batten Downingesque cottage that had been the very acme of architectural fashion before the Civil War.

Books like Sheldon's, and the generously illustrated magazines of the period, filled with drawings or photographs, were natural extensions of traditional pattern books. Among other things, they were showcases where provincial house builders and architects learned what was being built in more cosmopolitan places. The illustrations and articles in *American Architect and Building News*, especially, raised the level of professional taste and competence across many miles. For the most part the designs the magazines

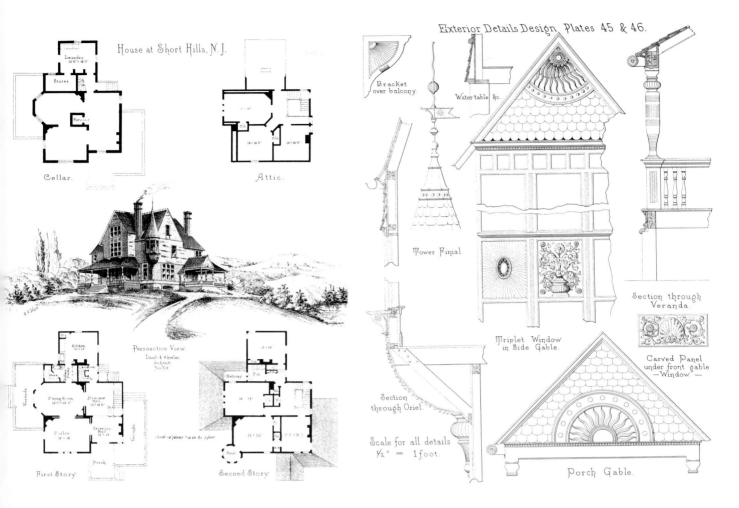

Fig. 153. (opposite) *Although its design vocabulary is familiar from pattern-book sources, the Anchorage is a high-style Queen Anne house that relies on the inventiveness of its architects.*

Fig. 154. (above, left) *Lamb and Wheeler, the architects of The Anchorage, were as well-known for educational institutions as they were for country houses. This is one of their more modest residential commissions.*

Fig. 155. (above, right) *The enlarged details from Lamb and Wheeler's Short Hills house were published in Comstock's* Modern Architectural Designs. *They served as inspiration and even as a directly copyable source for builders and rural architects in search of up-to-the-minute architectural fashion.*

Fig. 156. *A random-coursed stone first floor, shingled second floor, half-timbered third floor, shingled roof, and fluted chimney contribute textural complexity and distinguish this architect-designed Queen Anne house from more ordinary pattern-book examples. (Newark Public Library, Fine Arts Division)*

Fig. 157. *Like Thomas Edison's Glenmont, Charles W. McCutchen's expansive residence was typical of the upper-middle-class Queen Anne houses built in New Jersey's railroad suburbs during the 1880s.*

published during this period were unique creations, already built, but the ideas they conveyed were every bit as convincing as the information found in the more generic pattern book.

Unlike the limited circulation of Sheldon's book and the specialized appeal of *American Architect and Building News* was a periodical with a broad audience, a separate edition of the *Scientific American*. Called the *Architects and Builders Edition*, it was in the forefront of a movement that brought new architecture to a large public through cheap new printing techniques, including photography and improved color lithography. In the 1880s and 1890s its editors were partisans of the Queen Anne style. Many of their published examples came from New Jersey, not surprising since Orson D. Munn, publisher of the *Scientific American*, had lived in Llewellyn Park since 1870. "A Cottage at Monmouth Beach" (Fig. 159)

Fig. 158. The bell-roofed tower marks the far end of the McCutchen house in this photograph taken soon after its completion. Subsequent additions, compatible with the original design, centered the tower on the facade.

A Cottage at Monmouth Beach, N.J.   T. A. Roberts & Son, Architects, Newark, N.J.

Fig. 159. Color lithographs like this, from the Scientific American Architects and Builders Edition, *brought the public not only new architectural styles but also information about appropriate paint schemes and even landscaping ideas.*

was one of many vivid color lithographs the magazine printed, evidence of how far inexpensive printing for the mass market had come since the days of John Riddell's 1861 *Architectural Designs,* when color plates were a luxury. The Monmouth Beach lithograph illustrates the Queen Anne style at its most expansive and unbuttoned, evolving into the Shingle Style. The figures relaxing on the airy veranda and enjoying the ocean view from the second-floor porch symbolize the successful entrepreneurs of the Gilded Age reveling in one the fruits of their labors—fine architecture.

The owners of the cottage at Monmouth Beach hired the architectural firm T. A. Roberts and Son, of Newark, New Jersey.

Both client and architect might have been flattered to have the design published in a mass-circulation magazine. But the sizable house-building public that was reaching for solid middle-class consumer status, people like the butchers and plumbers of Maple Avenue in Madison, were probably unmoved by the propaganda of architects about what constituted good design, and whether they should seek it from pattern books, magazines, or from architects directly. In New Jersey the building boom of the 1880s and 1890s produced business enough for architects and pattern books alike. The Queen Anne house, with all of its Elizabethan, Jacobean, and even Japanese influences continued to be served up by a great variety of pattern books, with only slightly differing outlooks on the question of style. It was these publications that continued the practice of catering to the householder who aspired to something grander than a carpenter-designed cottage, but who stopped short of hiring an architect.

William Blair Titman was one of these. A typical self-made man, small-town variety, he was described as "one of Belvidere's most prominent and public-spirited citizens" (Fig. 160). He began life as a farmer and, following a post–Civil War pattern of success, grew prosperous from real estate speculation and banking. In 1891, at the age of forty-seven, he retired from farming and built a "beautiful home" in the town of Belvidere.[18] Titman showed off his success in business by building an asymmetrical, multi-gabled house, bedecked with lathe-turned spindles, posts, and porch friezes (Fig. 161).

Small-town man though he was, Titman was up to the minute in matters of architectural taste, thanks to pattern books. The design he chose came from a book published that same year, *The Cottage Souvenir No. 2*, by George F. Barber, another prolific architect-author of the late nineteenth century.[19] Like his contemporaries, Barber was stylistically versatile, but the designs most strongly associated with his work fall into a hybridized Queen Anne-Romanesque mode. Two of his favorite motifs were the Syrian (or horsehoe) arch and an oddly attentuated hipped roof that he often used on towers. Both of these can be seen in Design No. 53 (Fig. 162), which most closely matches the Titman house. "Most closely" is a reminder that Barber, like Palliser and Shoppell, whose mail-order services he emulated, encouraged his readers to "write to us concerning any changes wanted in the plans, and keep writing till you get just what you want. Don't be afraid of writing too often. We are not easily offended."[20] One of the simplest changes was to reverse the plan. Titman and his builder, a local carpenter named Reeder S. Emery, did just that.

By the 1890s, pattern books and their offspring, the journals and mass-circulation periodicals, were able to promote designs suitable for all tastes and pocketbooks. The eclectic Queen Anne

Fig. 160. *William Blair Titman, "one of Belvidere's most prominent and public spirited citizens." (*Cummins-Titman and Allied Families Genealogical Biographical, *by Anna Blair Titman Cummins, privately printed, 1946)*

Fig. 161. *The Titman house is readily identifiable as a product of George Barber's 1891 pattern book by its unusual tower roof and distinctive horseshoe arch on the front porch.*

PERSPECTIVE VIEW.

DESIGN No. 53.

Fig. 162. A visual riot of gables, peaks, turrets, and porches, this design was nonetheless described as "well proportioned," with a "grand entrance way [that] cannot fail to be admired by all," Its cost in 1891 was estimated at $5,250.

design that William Titman chose from the pages of *The Cottage Souvenir* was a purposely pretentious confection made feasible by new money and made possible by mass-produced millwork. At the same time, less-affluent builders could still find an array of designs to suit their needs. In December 1890, the *Scientific American Architects and Builders Edition* published a design for a cottage (Fig. 163) "built complete for a cost of twelve hundred dollars." It was a small house, to be sure, but the magazine's claim that it "has met with very general favor, and has been extensively copied" seems well founded. A version built in Riverdale (Fig. 164) appears to be one of the "modified examples" the description boasted of.

The popularity of designs by Shoppell, Palliser, Barber, and others insured that their books enjoyed long lives. Even as the Queen Anne gave way to the Shingle Style and then to the Colonial Revival at the turn of the century, older designs continued to be popular among working-class householders and those who were simply conservative. Shoppell's exhaustive *How to Build, Furnish, and Decorate* of 1883 featured many opulent Queen Anne houses, but its very first plate pictured a simple cross-gabled house that looked back to the 1860s (Fig. 165). This same house was built line for line in a Morristown neighborhood whose name, "Little Dublin," reflected its working-class character (Fig. 166).

Those intending to build, furnish, and decorate the suburban house had a substantial pattern-book literature to turn to by the end of the nineteenth century. The enormous influence of published sources on middle-class taste was summed up in 1894 by an architect named William A. Lambert. In *Suburban Architecture* Lambert explained:

> Previous to our own time homes capable of being constructed at a moderate cost made little or no claim to architectural pretensions, but . . . modest homes have been erected, which both for artistic effect as well as for comfort and convenience, have never been excelled in any previous time or country. . . . The designers of these homes have cast all architectural precedent to the winds, and finding nothing in the past of a similar character to which they could turn for inspiration, have returned to first principles, namely, convenience and natural use of materials, and the result is one in which truth and beauty assert themselves in combining to produce a structure which strives to be, and is in the fullest sense of the term, a home.[21]

Lambert documented houses built from his own designs in many New Jersey towns, among them Englewood, Hackensack, Passaic, and Paterson. His Design No. 235 (Fig. 167) suggests a

Fig. 163. Although the broad front gable with inset porch is no stranger to the late-nineteenth-century Queen Anne language of balconies and verandas, in this house it also foretells the early-twentieth-century bungalow.

Fig. 164. The encircling porch imparts an inviting summer-cottage-look to this year-round dwelling by extending the house into its landscape.

FRONT ELEVATION.

Fig. 165. Though published in 1883, this house reverts to a traditional side-hall-plan. Its centered cross-gable is symbol and summation of nearly four decades of pattern-book design.

transition between the Queen Anne and the Shingle Style and illustrates how the vigorously eclectic combinations that had characterized the work of Shoppell and Palliser in the 1880s had been simplified by the 1890s. To some extent it bore out Lambert's claim that designers had "cast all architectural precedent to the winds." Design No. 345 (Fig. 168) illustrates the architect's own house, built in Nutley. Features like a smoking room and servants' rooms in the attic made it larger than his other published designs, but it remained essentially what he described it as, a modest cottage, designed to be, "in the fullest sense of the term, a home."

Fig. 166. This simple house is an unusually direct copy of its pattern-book source. Even its slender chamfered columns have survived.

Smaller versions in several towns were adpated from Lambert's designs (Fig. 169).

All questions of style aside, the greatest achievement of the pattern books of the last quarter of the nineteenth century was the creation of suburbs full of middle-class homes where a larger number of people than ever before might, in Lambert's words, "enjoy the purer air and more pleasant surroundings of country life." Without pattern books and magazines, and architectural plans purchased through the mail, New Jersey's mass suburban transformation would never have taken place.

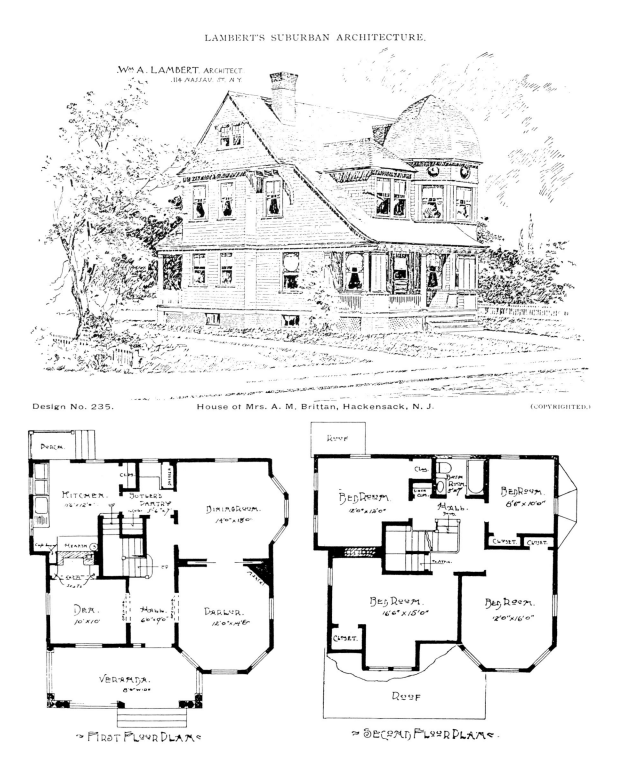

LAMBERT'S SUBURBAN ARCHITECTURE.

Wᵐ A. LAMBERT. ARCHITECT.
.114 NASSAU ST. N.Y.

Design No. 235.   House of Mrs. A. M. Brittan, Hackensack, N. J.   (COPYRIGHTED.)

Fig. 167. William Lambert's 1890s designs depicted spacious but not grandiose rooms and fashionable but unfussy exteriors.

Wᴹ A. LAMBERT..
..ARCHITECT...
.114. NASSAU ST NEW YORK..

Design No. 345.   Cottage of Mr. Wm. A. Lambert, Nutley, N. J.   (COPYRIGHTED.)

Fig. 168. The aproned maid seeing off mistress and child suggests a household run by servants. In reality, suburban families at the turn of the century were learning to manage without live-in help, a fact reflected in the simplification of designs by Lambert and his pattern-book contemporaries.

Fig. 169. A house in suburban Englewood bears the imprint of William Lambert.

Queen Anne Interiors

Fig. 170. Rossiter and Wright's living hall for an 1880 New Jersey house was long and narrow. It did, however, combine a fireplace and stairway, both requisites of the Queen Anne living hall.

If the exterior of the typical Queen Anne house—a collage of contrasting shapes and materials—was an eclectic tour de force, the ideal interior was a refined magpie's nest. For those who could afford it, the decor of the 1880s was a mélange of artifacts like Persian carpets, Japanese prints and fans, blue-and-white china from half a dozen different cultures, and motifs like the sunflower, the lily, and the owl, all popularized by the English Aesthetic Movement. The architectural frame for this exuberant domestic decoration was equally new and complex. The most avant garde

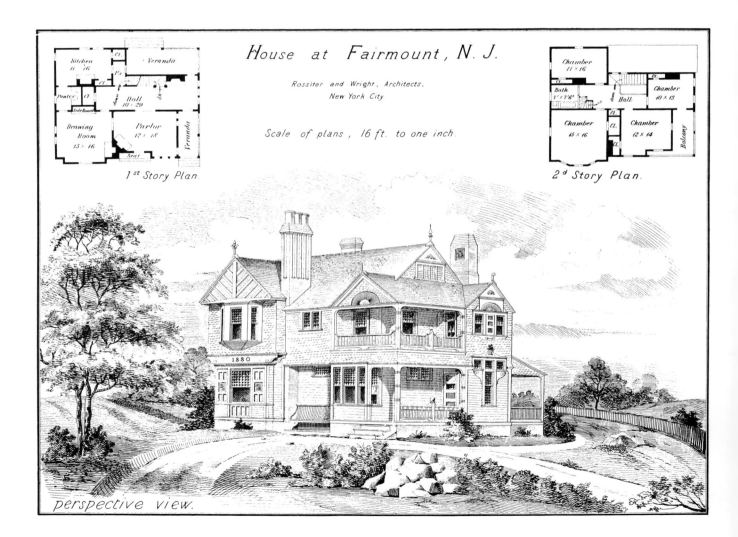

House at Fairmount, N.J.

Rossiter and Wright, Architects.
New York City

Scale of plans, 16 ft. to one inch.

1st Story Plan.

2d Story Plan.

perspective view.

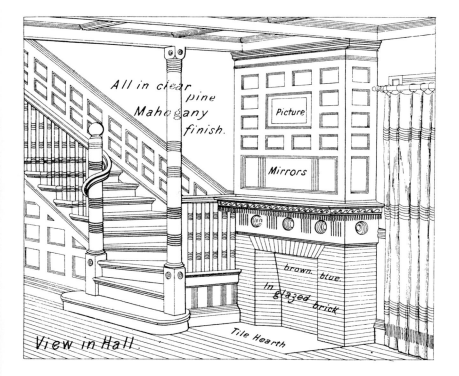

Fig. 171. Features like those pictured here became part of a formula for creating the fashionable living hall.

feature of the 1880s high-style house was the living hall. No longer a mere passageway with staircase, the living hall became a room in itself, the pivot point of the house and the primary place for impressing visitors.[22] A house (Fig. 170) designed by Rossiter and Wright for a client in Fairmount, New Jersey, and published in William Comstock's 1881 pattern book, *Modern Architectural Designs and Details*, depicted a long, narrow hall in transition toward the full-blown Queen Anne living hall. An accompanying vignette (Fig. 171) illustrated the two indispensable features of the living hall—staircase and fireplace—combined in the same room. Also pictured were such salient features as paneled walls and lathe-turned columns, an art-tile fireplace with paneled and mirrored overmantel, and to its right a doorway hung with portières.

By the time Charles H. Smith designed the McCutchen residence (see Fig. 158) in the mid-1880s, the living hall was the centerpiece of any high-style Queen Anne dwelling. As the plan shows (Fig. 172), Smith gave McCutchen his money's worth: a huge, angled mantel with inglenook bench beside it faced a staircase illuminated by a nineteen-by-seven-foot stained glass window, while more light poured into the richly paneled hall through wide doorways leading to three adjoining rooms.

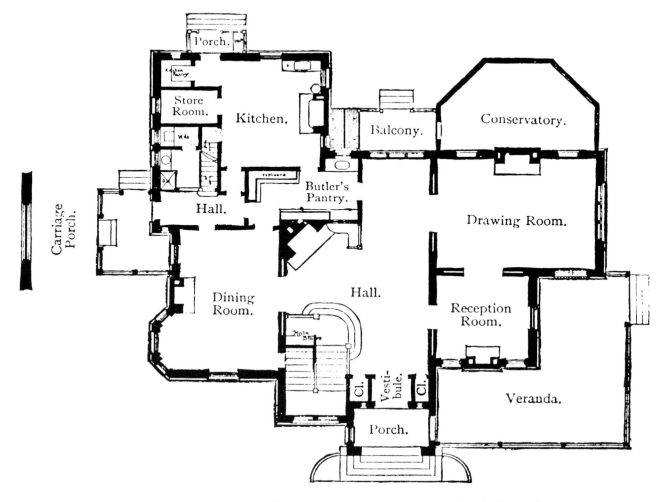

Fig. 172. The size and complexity of the high-style Queen Anne house is suggested by the plan for the McCutchen residence.

Henry Hudson Holly, always eager to clarify a point of design for his readers, analyzed interiors at length. Writing of a house he designed in Mountain Station and published in *Modern Dwellings* in 1878 (see Fig. 137), he observed that the staircase, fireplace, and bookcase built into its hall "give evidence of its being one of the living rooms." Whenever he pictured a living hall, Holly was sure to show staircase and fireplace together (Fig. 173).

A somewhat more middle-class interior pictured in Robert Shoppell's *Modern Houses* (1887) relied heavily on fabric hangings (Fig. 174). In fact, the original caption for this illustration was "A Plea for Portières." The glossy floors scattered with rugs, the hanging bookcase at the left (its own small portière drawn aside), the pottery massed on the mantel—all these were marks of the passion for fashionable nest-building that was common to householders of the 1880s.

William Titman's house (see Fig. 161) in Belvidere was documented in photographs that show a decorating scheme far simpler than the up-to-date *Cottage Souvenir* exterior might suggest, proof that building by the book was far from consistent in practice. But the generously draped portières between parlor and hall (Fig. 175) prove that even here, far from any cosmopolitan center, some bits of the pattern-book gospel of fashionable decor had been read and heeded.

Fig. 173. Henry Hudson Holly's interiors evidenced his interest in English design. The fireplace displays a Tudor arch; the mix of patterns on the walls reflects the influence of William Morris and the English Aesthetic Movement.

Fig. 174. Textiles were important to the Queen Anne interior. Ruminating on options, Robert Shoppell observed that "we have seen cretonne, heavy curtain stuff, Persian fabrics and decorated sail cloth in use. Sometimes plain and unadorned and again covered with embroidery or ornaments of brass, old coins, Japanese figures, or any of the thousand and one fashionable adornments of the day."

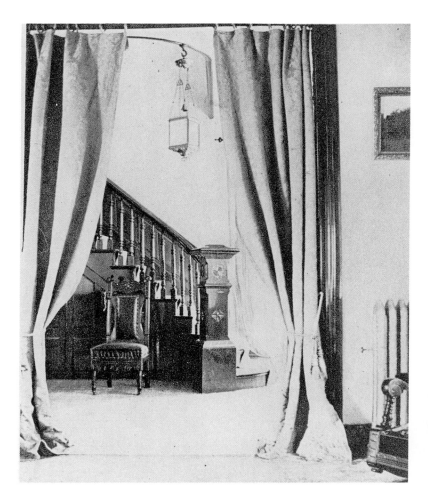

Fig. 175. William Titman decorated his house in a manner far simpler than Robert Shoppell advised, but he did use portières. (Cummins-Titman and Allied Families Genealogical Biographical, by Anna Blair Titman Cummins, privately printed, 1946)

Neighborhood Life

In the pattern-book neighborhood around Green and Maple avenues in Madison (see p. 156), houses with similar architecture created an atmosphere where small lots, although far from A. J. Downing's expansive suburban model, seem to have encouraged neighborliness instead of friction. A quarter of a century after many of the Maple Avenue houses were built, the well-established life of the neighborhood was reported in a *Madison Eagle* social column from 1917 that reflects the homely pleasures that the houses of the Co-operative Building Plan Association had helped foster:

> Attorney and Mrs. Frederick G. Watson have become permanent residents of Maple Avenue, having purchased the O'Brien house last week. Neighbors of the Watsons gave them a housewarming last Wednesday evening. . . . Mrs. Watson was presented a bag of kitchen utensils. Judge Schoneburger made the presentation. One of the highlights of the evening was the reading of a poem by Mr. Watson composed by Mr. Bush. Cards were enjoyed and refreshments served.

The houses built from pattern-book plans proved to be versatile. William F. Redmond, writing about his childhood in the 1889 house built for Judge Yeaman's family, recalled how well it served the rhythms of suburban life around the time of World War I, and recorded how his family used the house designed by Shoppell:

The bay window in the sitting room (our library) was really a bow window with five windows that opened up and down. The master bedroom above had a bow window the same size with a large built-in window seat which was cushioned. It was from there that I saw the big fire when the E. L. Cook Lumber Yard burned in 1916. The front bedroom was our upstairs sitting room. The third floor had three bedrooms. One over the master bedroom was the cook's. The one over the guest room was my play room. This contained, depending upon my age at the time, a rocking horse, electric trains, my chemical apparatus and even a small carpenter's workbench. The bedroom above the second floor sitting room was my sister's. She used it as her dressing room when she slept out on the open porch in the tower. All across the rear wing was a huge attic with a cedar-lined closet for winter clothes and blankets. At one end of the attic were many trunks and suitcases. The other end held window screens and porch shades in winter and the storm windows in summer. The front porch went around the side of the house. Most of the side porch was enclosed in glass and was Dad's conservatory where he raised many ferns. (Letter to Suzanne Benton, 10 January 1989)

The Importance of Porches

As early as 1850 Andrew Jackson Downing had observed, "No country house is tolerable in the United States without a veranda, arcade, or covered walk." Downing's successors took him at his word, agreeing that the porch was a nearly obligatory feature, and decades of pattern-book authors concocted countless variations on the porch theme. One of them, Henry Hudson Holly, wrote in 1863:

It is certainly our duty to introduce from abroad methods and manners of design, so far as meet our wants. But it would be worse than folly, in building an English cottage, for example, not to have a veranda, because its prototypes in England have none; we have an actual need for such an appliance in our dry and sunny climate, and it is out of such need that must proceed a distinctive feature of American cottage architecture.

By the time of his second pattern book, in 1878, Holly was designing "English cottage" (that is, Queen Anne) style porches (*opposite*) that were far more complex than the straightforward verandas of Downing's day.

No matter how complex, the porches of the 1880s and 1890s were composed most often from a range of columns, posts, brackets, and balusters readily available from local millwork shops, which might copy their products from a pattern book or offer their own interpretations of published designs. Typical were these veranda posts from a *Combined Book of Sash, Doors, Blinds and Moldings* (*below, left*), published in 1898. The balustrade at the left is nearly identical to the one at the right in Holly's drawing. The balustrade and spindled frieze together match a porch from a house of the same period in Lambertville (*below, right*).

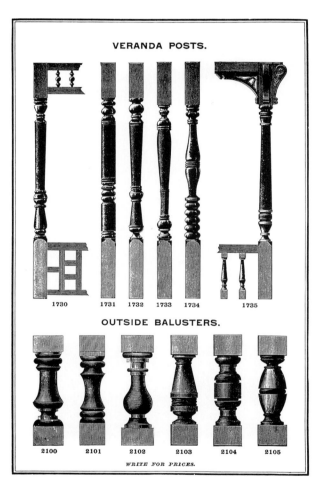

BACK TO BASICS

In our great cities we are hearing rumors of hard times, of people without employment, of children kept from school because they are not satisfactorily dressed, of high prices—that combination of evils which circulates from time to time in the vast metropolises of the world, but of which out in the country among the rural population there is very little talk.

The preceding quotation introduced an editorial titled "Small Farms a Solution for the Evils of Overcrowded Cities and Unnatural Living" published by Gustav Stickley in the June 1911 issue of *The Craftsman*. Despite its title, the editorial was about issues far larger than farming. Stickley was reexamining a dispute current in American intellectual discourse since at least the writings of Thomas Jefferson. It was an argument that Stickley's contemporary Frank Lloyd Wright would also engage: agrarianism versus urbanism.

Like Jefferson and Wright, Stickley put his faith in the purity of the rural-suburban environment and its ability to function as a

Fig. 176. The trolley, and even more force-fully, the automobile, shaped suburban de-velopment—its location, its layout, and its extent—in the twentieth century. (John Steen, Mountain Lakes Landmarks Committee)

Fig. 177. Houses under construction at Mountain Lakes, New Jersey, about 1910. This early-twentieth-century development was marked by a progressive attitude to-ward architecture, family life, and the en-vironment. (John Steen, Mountain Lakes Landmarks Committee)

Fig. 178. As the twentieth century dawned, the idea of suburbia evolved from one of iso-lated country homes to entire communities. Recreational lakes, golf courses, and pub-licly accessible open space became sought-after amenities. (John Steen, Mountain Lakes Landmarks Committee)

matrix for democracy. This city-country struggle emerged again just as New Jersey was feeling the pressure of intensified development spreading out from the urban cores of Manhattan and Philadelphia and from its own cities. By the beginning of the twentieth century the state's original railroad suburbs were well established. The arrival of interurban trolley lines, followed by the gradual adoption of the automobile, enabled suburban development patterns to grow more flexible (Fig. 176).

While the small-town commuter railroad station remained an important locus of residential growth, the new means of transportation gave fresh energy to suburbanization. Developers played on the kind of antiurban sentiment expressed in Stickley's editorial as they laid out new communities on cheap land at greater distances from the old points of railroad convenience. One of them was Watson Whittlesey, who began building Livingston Manor in 1908 on a rise above the Raritan River, overlooking the city of New Brunswick. Whittlesey was quick to seize an opportunity, for the borough of Highland Park had been incorporated only three years earlier on land that had been exclusive villa sites in the nineteenth century. His marketing prospectus emphasized the trolley loop that ran down to the city, making it possible for residents to shop or work in New Brunswick, or to catch the train there for more distant points. Whittlesey's estimate of suburban euphoria was accurate. Between 1910 and 1920 the population of Highland Park sprang from 1,500 to 4,866.

Farther north, far from an urban concentration like New Brunswick, another developer was carving roads and building lots from much rougher terrain (Fig. 177). In 1910 Herbert Hapgood began creating what eventually became the Borough of Mountain Lakes, on the border of Boonton. Like Whittlesey, Hapgood based his development's appeal on the desire for a domestic environment surrounded by the natural world. Dramatically rural, his new community was characterized by its eponymous lakes (Fig. 178). But along the Boulevard, its main avenue, ran a trolley line that connected Mountain Lakes to its more developed neighbors. In 1912 Hapgood saw to it that a picturesque stone railroad station was built, providing a convenient connection to New York. Garages were not a standard feature, but the private automobile soon became common in Mountain Lakes.

Growing out of antiurbanism and fueled by improved means of transportation, this fresh wave of suburban development was colored by an altered social and economic structure and smaller family size. All of these conditions needed a new kind of architecture and a spokesman for a new set of values.

VOL. XXII, No. 1   APRIL, 1912   25 CENTS

THE CRAFTSMAN

"The lyf so short, the craft so long to lerne."

THE BETRAYAL OF THE
PEOPLE BY A FALSE
DEMOCRACY:
BY GUTZON BORGLUM

VALUE TO OUR NATION
OF THE VANISHING
WATER BIRDS

PERGOLAS AS
SCREENS FOR
TOWN AND VIL-
LAGE HOMES

HOW THE ARCHITECT
MAY HELP SOLVE ECO-
NOMIC AND SOCIAL
PROBLEMS

A FRIENDLY GARDEN
WITH PICTURESQUE
FEATURES AND MANY
FLOWERS

THE WILD GARDENS OF
CALIFORNIA

FLOWERS FOR THE
ROCK GARDEN

HERBS FOR AN OLD-
FASHIONED GARDEN

FORTY-ONE-WEST-THIRTY-FOURTH-STREET-NEW-YORK

Fig. 179. The Craftsman *helped popularize the Arts and Crafts philosophy of simplicity in home furnishings and design.*

Stickley's Revolution

In 1908 New Jersey's rural landscape drew Gustav Stickley from Syracuse, New York. Not far from Herbert Hapgood's string of lakes he bought six hundred acres of abandoned farmland. There, in Morris Plains (now Parsippany), he began building a home, a model farm, and what he hoped would become a school. Stickley's intention to create a refuge from urban ills was appreciated by a visitor to Craftsman Farms in 1910, who wrote, "An hour's railroad journey had released [him] from the turmoil of the metropolis on a hot June day, and a short drive had brought him to this peaceful spot, where, as though in quiet defiance of the discordant roar of the city, the deep green of the forest's 'talking leaves' seemed to repeat that no life were truly life, no wisdom truly wise without the 'open world' and the teachings of nature."[1]

Stickley had first gained public attention as the designer and manufacturer of furniture often called Mission, but his vision encompassed far more than furniture. In 1901, he had begun publishing *The Craftsman*, a monthly magazine devoted to reformist ideas in everything from home design to city planning (Fig. 179). Starting in 1903, every issue contained two designs for "Craftsman Homes." Included were plans, one or two perspective drawings, sometimes interior views, and a narrative description that included treatment of building materials, siting, and other essential features. *Craftsman* subscribers could order, at no cost, blueprints for one of these houses. Readers responded with such enthusiasm that in 1909 Stickley brought out *Craftsman Homes*, a collection of plans that had appeared in the magazine, followed three years later by *More Craftsman Homes*.

Serial publication of house designs for later collection was a practice familiar on the American scene since the work of Samuel Sloan and William Ranlett in the 1850s; in the 1880s Shoppell and the Pallisers had proven the mass appeal of house plans by mail. What, then, was so revolutionary about Stickley's approach?

Like his Craftsman furniture, Stickley's Craftsman homes were a conscious response to what the English and eventually the American Arts and Crafts movement perceived as the debilitating effects of industrialized production and the distancing of the worker from his craft—"Nowadays, you never see the man who made your chairs, and he never sees you," complained Stickley. As we saw in chapter four, the ideal house for middle-class Americans in the 1880s and 1890s was the Queen Anne cottage merchandised so successfully by the Co-operative Building Plan Association and other pattern-book publishers whose dwellings filled New Jersey suburbs. For aesthetic appeal these houses relied on painted polychromy and mass-produced decorative millwork. By contrast—and a dramatic contrast it was—Stickley's goal was "a fine plainness."

His effort to relate domestic architecture to its landscape surroundings and to rid it of superfluous ornament resulted not so much in an easily identifiable style as an attitude about houses. The Craftsman house was simple and forthright. Most often it displayed little or no debt to any historical style. On the exterior, Stickley preferred either site-specific wood and stone or innovative materials like poured concrete and hollow tile. Inside, he carried to its logical end the simplification of planning that had begun to evolve at the end of the nineteenth century. His houses, mostly small, featured efficient plans free of wasteful corridors, halls, or formal parlors; built-in furniture was incorporated wherever possible (an odd strategy for a furniture manufacturer, as several historians have pointed out). Central to every house was a large fireplace, often with inglenook seats, where the family could gather (Fig. 180). His insistence on the value of the hearth was found in virtually all of Stickley's designs and underlined his belief in the metaphoric power of the house:

A home without a hearth—is it not a body without a soul? We Americans thought we had done a fine practical thing when we tore the hearth from the family living room and buried the fire, a thing of beauty and inspiration, in the cellar! The furnace is of course a necessity to city life, yet I believe that the absence

Fig. 180. *This interior detail of a house published in* The Craftsman *in June 1901 has all of Stickley's hallmarks: a rustic stone fireplace with broad hearth; a built-in seat or "inglenook"; and built-in bookcases beneath grouped casement windows.*

of the family hearth has done more than any single thing to destroy the home feeling in the American household.[2]

Because he wanted his designs to serve real domestic needs, Stickley encouraged readers to become full participants in the planning and execution of their homes. In 1913 he had this to say about design alterations initiated by a homeowner for a house built in New Jersey:

Naturally, we are more than pleased when an owner takes such a personal interest in the various features of construction and arrangement. And the more closely we can cooperate with him in working out all the details and embodying his ideas in practical form, the more satisfied we are both likely to be with the final result. For when a home is planned with such close relation to the family needs and the nature of the site, a good deal of comfort and picturesqueness are apt to result.[3]

Prospective suburbanites everywhere were taking to heart Stickley's views. Like many businessmen, Edmond Diefenthaler, president of the Astor Coffee Company, was eager to escape New York City. In a letter to Adalene Cook, his fiancée, he told of making an exploratory trip to the countryside beyond the Hudson River:

Chatham appears to be a pretty little place. Struck a spot not too far from the depot that has a beautiful location on top of the mountain. The air must be good and healthy. I have always liked to dream of a living room in my home where there would be a built-in bookcase, open fireplace, Mission trimming, beamed ceiling, etc. I was wondering whether this combination would appeal to your own ideals, sweetheart?[4]

Adalene said yes to marriage and to Edmond's architectural fancies. In 1909 they completed their house, filled with precisely the Arts and Crafts features Edmond had imagined, with porch and chimney built with several tons of rock blasted from the site.

Although Stickley's own house at Craftsman Farms (Fig. 181) was a dramatic illustration of his theories, it was unique, not intended for direct emulation. None of Stickley's records survive to tell us how many readers built houses from designs published in *The Craftsman*, but the popularity of his two collections of plans suggests that there were many. This lack of documentation, the likelihood of creative deviation from the published designs, and the fact that Craftsman houses are usually more distinctive inside than out have frustrated the effort to document built examples. Two of the New Jersey houses that have been identified illustrate

Fig. 181. Stickley's own house at Craftsman Farms, built in 1908, is an exagger-ated version of the log cabin of the American past, symbolizing the agrarian, democratic virtues that Stickley feared mass-production was erasing.

Stickley's design values and the manner in which readers used his plans.

The December 1910 issue of the *The Craftsman* featured two designs under the headline "Craftsman Houses for Small Fami-lies." The accompanying text noted:

> Both the designs we publish this month show houses that are small, simple and inexpensive, being meant to suit the needs of small families with moderate means. But while the cost

has been kept down to the minimum for a properly built Craftsman house, both these little dwellings are solidly built, comfortable and as attractive as any houses we have ever designed.[5]

One of these two, House No. 104, was later published in *More Craftsman Homes* as a "Moderate-Sized Brick House, with Recessed Porch and Pleasant, Homelike Rooms" (Fig. 182). In addition to its brick walls, the materials specified were V-jointed cypress boards for the attic story, and a slate roof. The plan reveals Stickley's favorite living room focal point, the inglenook. According to the text, "The whole end of the living room is occupied by the big fireplace nook shown in the illustration. This forms the chief structural feature of the house and also gives the keynote of color."

Soon after this design's publication in *The Craftsman*, a house was built from it in Oradell, then known as Delford, a sparsely settled Bergen County suburb about ten miles west of New York City. Helen May Vaill and her husband, Edward W. Vaill, Jr., followed Stickley's advice and adapted the design to suit their needs without altering its character (Fig. 183). First, they reversed the plan to create a mirror image of the original, probably for siting reasons. Instead of building with brick, they used hollow tile (a patented fireproof material often advertised in *The Craftsman*) covered with cement stucco, and substituted clay tile for the suggested roof slates. A few minor changes in dimensions and window and door arrangement (one change was designed to make more wall space for the family piano) completed their revisions.

The excitement of collaborating on a home design in a new suburb was recalled by the Vaill's daughter, who "remembers her parents moving to Oradell from Englewood, New Jersey and living in a rented home down the hill from the plot where their new home was being built. She remembers her father and mother poring over the blueprints which were pasted to the living room wall. Every evening they went up the hill to watch the progress of the construction."[6] The Vaills seem to have been the embodiment of Stickley's ideal homeowners. Edward Vaill was an attorney, the personification of the professional whose education equipped him to appreciate the virtues of a Craftsman home. The fact that he worked in Manhattan but lived in the suburbs was proof of Stickley's belief that the working man needed a cozy retreat surrounded by greenery to revive his spirits. The Vaills and their son and daughter constituted the small family for which this four-bedroom house was the perfect home. It was entered in the municipal tax rolls in December 1911, one year after it was published in *The Craftsman*.

A second Craftsman house documented to a New Jersey location was built in Morris Plains (Fig. 184), not far from Stickley's own home at Craftsman Farms. Published in April 1913 as Crafts-

Fig. 182. Published in The Craftsman *in December 1910 as "House No. 104," this design is unusual in its use of brick instead of cement or stucco, which Stickley espoused as the more "modern" materials of home building.*

Fig. 183. Reversed in plan from the design in The Craftsman, *the Vaill House is otherwise a faithful example of its published prototype.*

man House No. 157 (Fig. 185), it was designed for W. C. Parker, a professional photographer. Stickley and Parker were friends. In fact, the same issue of *The Craftsman* included an article about how a Craftsman interior was designed for the Parker Photographic Studio in Morristown. The personal connection makes it probable that this was one of the houses for which Stickley himself was the principal designer, although no documentation has been found. Like the house for the Vaills, the Parker house has a simple, open plan that survives unaltered. Unlike many Craftsman houses, it features a separate entry hall with staircase, and its large fieldstone fireplace occupies the long wall of the living room without an inglenook. As if to corroborate his own belief in the importance of siting and the desirability of site-specific materials, Stickley accompanied the design with these remarks about Parker's approach to building the house:

> As the owner was particularly fond of field stone and had plenty of it on his site, he naturally decided to use it for the first story. . . . This house was planned for a western exposure, so that the living porch at the side would face the south. But if others wished to build from this design and the lot happened to front on the east, a southern exposure could still be retained for the living porch by simply reversing the plan.

Parker was a prominent man in his community and, like his friend Gustav Stickley, was both an artist and a businessman. His more than ordinary interest in the Craftsman style notwithstanding, Parker's house was identical in its essentials to the great run of houses published in *The Craftsman*, and very similar in size and detailing to the Vaill house. This fact underlines Stickley's egalitarian architectural goals. Although he published a few larger and more pretentious Craftsman houses, his designs were not intended for a display of conspicuous consumption; on the contrary, they were the most consistent examples America had yet seen of domestic architecture for the thinking middle class. An examination of the Parker and Vaill houses reveals another revolutionary aspect of Stickley's architecture—its lack of reference to historical precedents. In plan and elevation neither house displays any discernible clues to American or European models. Although Stickley published with admiration the work of Americans like Wilson Eyre and Englishmen like Barry Parker and Raymond Unwin, architects who did not reject historical inspiration entirely, his own designs made only infrequent and passing reference to such sources.

Stickley's deep commitment to organic architecture took the place of reliance on historical models. His houses were designed from the inside out in a manner that put function first. The way a house was meant to be used and the presumed values of its owners

Fig. 184. Named "Silver Birch" by its original owners, the Parkers, Craftsman House No. 157 is now almost hidden by those same trees.

Fig. 185. Shingle siding above a stone base may recall Queen Anne architecture, but in this Craftsman house, the materials provide the only "decoration" and integrate the building with its site.

dictated its appearance more than traditional ideas about class, social hierarchy, and economic status. For these reasons it was difficult to impress one's neighbors with a Craftsman house on anything but intellectual grounds, a decidedly revolutionary idea in American architecture.

Stickley was not the only reformer who pressed Arts and Crafts ideals on the American public, but his comprehensive presentation of the movement in all its manifestations through the pages of *The Craftsman* made him its most influential advocate. The number of New Jersey houses built directly from *Craftsman* designs is unknown, but Stickley's influence is potent even when measured by the houses he influenced indirectly. One example is Watson Whittlesey's development, begun only five years after Stickley published his first designs for Craftsman houses. Although the individual houses at Livingston Manor display stylistic variety, and even some traces of historicism, the perspective of eighty years makes it evident that their size and scale, their details and materials are all imbued with the Arts and Crafts attitude. More specifically, individual features abound that resemble details of published *Craftsman* designs. Pergolas, for example, were a typical Craftsman feature, designed to enhance the connection between indoors and out. Whittlesey's own cement house (Fig. 186) displays a pergola entrance much like Stickley's design No. 74, a cement house "with cement pillars and pergola construction above" (Fig. 187).

As a rule, Herbert Hapgood's houses for Mountain Lakes are larger than Whittlesey's or Stickley's. Some are dressed up with historical ornament, but without Stickley's influence most would not look the way they do. Many of their interiors might have been lifted directly from the pages of *The Craftsman* (Fig. 188). Chestnut paneling, beamed ceilings, and plate rails were treated in the plain Craftsman manner—despite the irony that these spacious houses were designed to be maintained by servants. At least one Hapgood house (Fig. 189), built about 1910, was taken directly from a design first published in *The Craftsman* in January 1904. Built as house "A" in the Hapgood development, it differs from the published design in the reversal of its floor plan and the substitution of a full, open porch across the facade, rather than one enclosed at either end (Fig. 190). When Stickley reissued the design for this house as part of his first pattern-book collection, *Craftsman Homes*, he took pains to remind readers that "the design as shown here is clearly suggestive in nature, making clear the fundamental principles of the Craftsman house and leaving room for such variation of detail as the owner may desire."

Gustav Stickley's designs for furniture and houses stood in the service of a larger program, nothing less than the reform of American family life for its central role in a democracy. Like William Morris, to whom the first issue of *The Craftsman* was dedicated,

Fig. 186. The massive piers and exposed rafter ends of this Highland Park portico give expression to the Arts and Crafts belief in architectural simplicity and the honesty of materials.

DETAIL VIEW OF CRAFTSMAN CEMENT FARMHOUSE NO. 74, SHOWING FRONT ENTRANCE WITH CEMENT PILLARS AND PER-GOLA CONSTRUCTION ABOVE. THE SIMPLE BUT EFFECTIVE TREATMENT OF THE DOOR AND SMALL CASEMENTS ON EITHER SIDE IS ALSO WORTH NOTICING.

Fig. 187. This detail of a pergola porch was published in the September 1909 issue of The Craftsman. *The accompanying text stated that "the vine over the pergola and the flower boxes set between the pillars add a note of grace and hospitality to the entrance, and seem to knit the house more closely to its surroundings."*

Fig. 188. The interior of a Craftsman-inspired house in Mountain Lakes shows the strong articulation of structural and quasi-structural members. (John Steen, Mountain Lakes Landmarks Committee)

Stickley believed that every aspect of the home was worthy of the artist's attention. He was convinced that well-designed furniture, houses, gardens, and larger environments would foster the values by which Americans ought to live. Like the recurrent dispute over agrarianism versus urbanism, this program was not new in American intellectual life. Wherever we look in the writing of Andrew Jackson Downing more than half a century earlier, we find firm foundations for Stickley's thought. Both emphasized the importance of beautiful surroundings in everyday life and the recuperative power of nature. Both believed, in Downing's words, that "unostentatious, moderate homes" were essential to a nation of democrats. With only a few adjustments, Stickley's 1909 foreword to *Craftsman Homes* might just as easily have been written by Downing: "Fundamental principles . . . underlie the planning of every Craftsman house. These principles are simplicity, durability,

Fig. 189. The broad and open front porch looked down to the boat launch of a man-made lake when this house, and the Mountain Lakes community in which it stands, were new in 1910. (John Steen, Mountain Lakes Landmarks Committee)

Fig. 190. The January 1904 issue of The Craftsman *in which this house was published described it as being in the California Mission Style. With only a few changes Herbert Hapgood built the same house in Mountain Lakes and called it "Moorish," perhaps for the stuccoed porch arches.*

fitness for the life that is to be lived in the house and harmony with its natural surroundings. Given these things, the beauty and comfort of the home environment develops as naturally as a flowering plant from the root."

Both Downing and Stickley were influenced by a nation where social relationships, population centers, building practices, and technology were changing rapidly. Downing's pattern books helped create New Jersey's suburbs; Stickley's magazine and two house pattern books helped to edge those suburbs a little closer to the egalitarian spirit Downing had espoused but had failed to achieve in practice.

Houses by Mail

Just as other architects and pattern-book authors had used Downing's work to fashion a new vernacular architecture, Stickley's work was used almost immediately in the same way. His imitators brought Craftsman-like houses to an audience that was larger than the one reached by his own publications. The popularization of the small, practical house based on Craftsman principles resulted from a combination of marketing and technology proposed earlier but never fully developed.

The idea for mass-produced housing had been suggested by several ninteenth-century writers who reasoned that the factory system that could make inexpensive clothing, furniture, and shoes should be able to do the same for buildings. The first full-blown statement of that aim in American pattern-book literature might be dated to 1856, when C. P. Dwyer's *Economic Cottage Builder* proposed that "perhaps it might not be altogether out of place to suggest the practicability of a scheme which might be highly useful to the community. . . . It is to establish sawmills and planing machines . . . where all the parts of a complete building could be worked up and carried piece-meal to market, every joint appropriately numbered and all got ready for setting up in any locality."

As we have seen already, there arose in the last quarter of the nineteenth century a whole class of successful entrpreneurs who sold house plans by mail. Although these mail-order plans were cheaper than consulting with an architect, the home builder still had to hire a carpenter to build the house, so construction itself remained a handcrafted operation. Around 1900 the Gordon-Van Tine Company took an important step forward. It offered through its catalogs complete blueprints by mail and from its warehouse many of the house components that the plans specified. Ready-

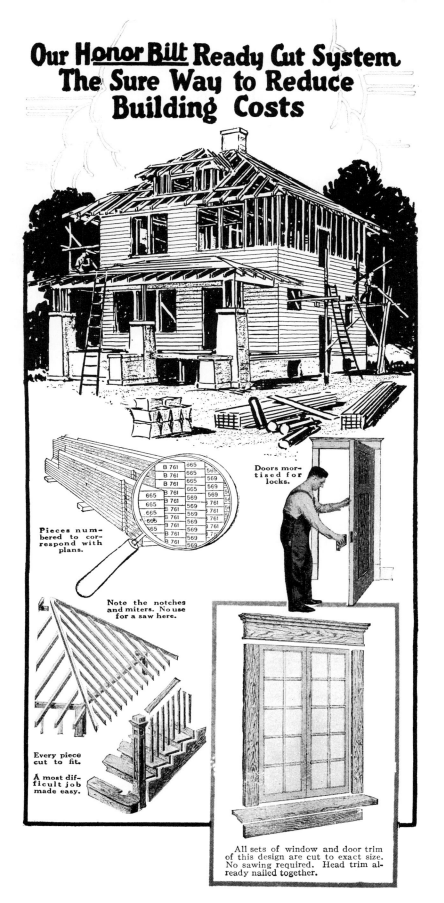

Fig. 191. Advertisements for "ready-cut" houses assured potential builders of the quality of construction and coupled a modern method with modern styling. (Sears, Roebuck and Company)

made doors, windows, stairs, and porch members had been available before, but Gordon-Van Tine's pairing of these components with the plans that called for them made the crucial connection necessary for the growth of the ready-cut housing industry.

Although several companies had produced prefabricated houses before the Civil War, the first successful offer of complete build-it-yourself houses by mail was made by the Aladdin Company of Bay City, Michigan. Aladdin, founded in 1904, was followed a few years later by Sears, Roebuck and Company, which quickly became the largest manufacturer of catalog houses (Fig. 191). Because the industry developed when it did, many of its early designs fell into the Arts and Crafts mode. The fact that Stickley's first Craftsman designs were published in 1903 and his first pattern book appeared in 1909, just as the industry was hitting its stride, makes comparisons inevitable. In 1913 Sears introduced a model called the Westly (Fig. 192). Its roofline and porch were clumsy by comparison with Stickley's Craftsman House No. 63 (Fig. 193), but the exteriors were similar overall, and shared a balconied dormer of almost identical design. The most significant difference is found inside. Stickley created a typically open Craftsman plan with three large rooms and an inglenook fireplace. In the Sears version four boxy rooms are disposed around a traditional center hall. No documentation exists to prove whether House No. 63 was built, but Sears, Roebuck records show that the Westly was built in Vineland. It was undoubtedly built in many other New Jersey towns as well; one example is found in Hasbrouck Heights (Fig. 194).

Their designers called the Westly and Craftsman House No. 63 bungalows. During the teens of the twentieth century the bungalow became an appealing alternative for moderate-income families from coast to coast, the answer to the search for a simple home that would be easy to maintain and would mirror the modern, more casual life of its inhabitants. The bungalow's popularity prompted even very old dogs to learn new tricks. The Co-operative Building Plan Association, established in 1877 and responsible for so many Queen Anne cottages (see Fig. 149), had by the beginning of the new century become the Co-operative Architects. Their June 1908 issue of *Shoppell's Owners and Builders Magazine* ($1.50 a year) was a "Special Bungalow Number," filled with up-to-date designs. The September issue for the same year featured a bungalow with an inglenook, "which has become a necessity for the modern country home." As early as 1910 *Keith's Magazine* published an article devoted to "Historical Aspects of the Bungalow," which, its author maintained, "is stamping our architecture with an adaptability and adjustment that is as ingenious as the American himself."

The true bungalow is a one-story house with a low-pitched roof extending over a front porch, although one-and-one-half and even small two-story houses often acquired the bungalow label. Like Stickley's Craftsman houses, the best bungalows were typi-

Fig. 192. The Westly was a bungalow introduced by Sears, Roebuck only a few years after Gustav Stickley published a similar house. (Sears, Roebuck, and Company)

Fig. 193. Called a farmhouse when it appeared in The Craftsman *in 1909, this bungalow inspired suburban houses across New Jersey.*

Fig. 194. This well-preserved example of the Westly needs only the replacement of its balcony railing to match the catalogue illustration.

fied by informality, compact plans, and the use of natural materials, but the bungalow itself always remained a house type rather than a style.[7]

Bungalows in various stylistic dress accounted for a large percentage of the catalog-house business. No design sums up bungalow characteristics better than Aladdin's Pomona, which appeared in the company's catalog for 1918–1919 (Fig. 195). Broad and low, with deep sheltering eaves and front porch, the Pomona was clad in wood shingles with frame trim. Aladdin and Sears offered many similar bungalows with almost identical floor plan but different elevations. Aladdin frequently invoked California associations for its bungalows, while claiming they were every bit as suitable for wintry climates. Since most bungalows featured living rooms entered directly from outside without hall or vestibule, that claim seems questionable, but Aladdin had no trouble selling its bungalows in New Jersey. One well-preserved example of the Pomona in Madison is identical to the catalog illustration but for the use of cobblestones in place of brick for the chimney and porch piers (Fig. 196). Built in a neighborhood that was opened for development in 1917, this house first appeared on a 1921 map, three years after its first catalog publication.

Thanks to both their appearance, which is consistent with the published sources, and the company's accessible records, Sears bungalows built in New Jersey are easier to identify than their Stickley-inspired counterparts. In 1916 Sears introduced a model called the Osborn, which it kept in production for thirteen years (Fig. 197). The catalog note combines simple description with clever but low-key promotion:

> Bungalow authorities agree that this type of architecture has come to stay. They claim that as the years go by the bungalow will be even in more demand than at the present time, and should one wish to sell he will have little difficulty in finding a buyer. While the Osborn is neither extreme nor extravagant, it has all the earmarks of a cozy, well-planned, artistic home. The stuccowork of the porches, with red brick coping, the gables and chimneys at once draw the attention of the passerby.

Not only does this brief paragraph invoke "bungalow authorities" to guarantee resale value, it uses the words "cozy" and "artistic" to play on the public's simultaneous desire for domestic and aesthetic fulfillment, two leitmotifs of the Arts and Crafts movement, interpreted here for a large market of bungalow buyers. As to "well-planned," the floor plan was indeed ingenious. Typical of the Sears true bungalow, where all rooms were confined to one floor, the layout runs a double rank of rooms behind a large living

Fig. 195. The Pomona, one of the Aladdin Company's most popular models of the 1910s, was designed to "radiate the delightful California sunniness and typify the bungalow-craft."

Fig. 196. Aladdin Readi-Cut Houses were economical, stylish, and backed by the company's "Dollar-A-Knot Guarantee," which promised to reimburse the purchaser one dollar for each knot found. One of the well-built results is this Pomona in Madison.

FROM THE GOLDEN WEST

The OSBORN
Honor Bilt
$2,192.00

See Description of "Honor Bilt" Houses on Page 9.

No. 2050 "Already Cut" and Fitted.

Living Room

*T*HIS modern and spacious compartment extends the entire width of the house. Note the bookcase colonnade and the brick mantel. The fortunate owner will find this room a most inviting and comfortable retreat.

Dining Room

*T*HIS room is provided with a beamed ceiling, massive buffet, plate rail and panel strips. French doors lead into the private side porch.

Read the full description of the Osborn "Honor Bilt" Modern Home on the opposite page.

SEARS ROEBUCK AND CO. CHICAGO

Fig. 198. *Today we see the Osborn as a bungalow with a decidedly Japanese design influence in both the stacked rafters above the high porch piers and the curiously peaked gable ends.*

room, which takes up the entire width of the house behind the front porch. The kitchen and two bedrooms are reached by walking through the dining room, so that only a tiny hall is needed in front of the bathroom. In reality the house is a rectangle, but its shape is disguised by a second porch off the dining room, which imparts a feeling of openess to an otherwise tight plan.

The Osborn's Japanese influence is nowhere commented on, perhaps because generalized Japanese features were taken for granted in bungalow design by this date. Instead the catalog mentions "colonial windows" and a "Craftsman front door." The interior is explicitly Craftsman in feeling, with large brick fireplace, built-in bookcases and buffet, beamed ceiling, and plate rail; even Craftsman-type lanterns are hung from the ceiling. It seems that "Craftsman" had become thoroughly generic by 1916, just as Stickley's *Craftsman* magazine was about to succumb to its creator's bankruptcy. Like every one of the more popular Sears models, this mildly exotic bungalow was built in numerous New Jersey towns. High Bridge has an Osborn. So do Pequannock (Fig. 198) and Morris Township (Fig. 199).

More than mildly exotic was a design for an overtly Japanesque "three-story bungalow" published in 1910 in *Bungalow Magazine*, another influential design source. The cover illustration

Fig. 199. *One New Jersey builder used cobblestones to give the Osborn a textural richness the stucco-walled catalog illustration never had.*

Fig. 197. *(opposite) Like Aladdin's Pomona, Sears stressed the California origins of the Osborn by advertising it as "From the Golden West" when it was introduced in the catalog of 1916. (Sears, Roebuck, and Company)*

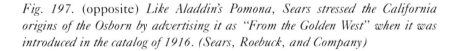

Everything *and* the Kitchen Sink

Factory-built housing purveyors like Aladdin, Harris Brothers, and Sears, Roebuck claimed to offer everything needed for home construction—and their claims were true. Architectural plans, detailed instructions, and lumber precut and marked were the basic essentials. By manufacturing and distributing in large quantities, they could also offer window glass, hardware, plumbing, roofing, and paint at competitive prices.

House kits were shipped by boxcar, and about the only things the manufacturer could not provide were masonry and the cellar. A contractor or the owner could put the pieces together. Advertising, like this 1921 Sears copy, encouraged the do-it-yourself approach: "You will enjoy building the Crescent. The construction is very simple. We furnish of course all necessary blueprints and instructions. You simply can't go wrong. Any of the homes shown in this catalog can be built in just a few days' time."

Sears, especially, was a complete domestic outfitter. Buyers of a Sears ready-cut house could arrange to purchase everything they needed—including the kitchen sink. Sears, of course, was also eager to sell the new homeowner furniture, pots and pans, and clothes to hang in the closets. According to Katherine Cole Stevenson and H. Ward Jandl, authors of *Houses by Mail*, "Sears apparently was successful in selling houses and furnishings as a single package." In the words of a 1939 Sears advertisement, "In many instances, homes have been built for customers who bought all of their home equipment and home furnishings at the local Sears retail store."

There are several reasons for the large number of Sears houses in New Jersey. For one thing, plentiful rail connections made shipment easy, but perhaps just as important were the presence of a regional sales office in Trenton and a forty-acre lumber mill in Newark. Whatever the reasons, Sears had satisfied New Jersey customers by the hundreds. In their comprehensive history of the Sears housing achievement, Stevenson and Jandl quote Richard Ferguson, of Linden, who captured the all-important personal connection between house and builder in these words:

Our home, the Cornell, was built in 1918. My dad did the carpentry and subcontracted the masonry, electrical and plumbing work. I recall the times during my folks' later years when my mother suggested they sell and buy a retirement home at the Jersey shore. My dad's reply was always the same: "I built this house. I know where every nail is. It's a good, solid house and I'm not leaving it." And neither of them did.

One Order Brings It All

Lumber, Lath and Shingles

Millwork

WHEN YOU PURCHASE A HOUSE FROM SEARS, ROEBUCK AND CO.

You dispose of the entire transaction in a few minutes. You select your house from our Book of "Honor Bilt" Modern Homes, merely writing down the name or number, and on receipt of your order we ship at the prices quoted.

THE LUMBER,
   LATH AND
      SHINGLES;
      MILL WORK, SUCH AS
         DOORS,
            WINDOWS,
               MOLDING,
                  BUILDING PAPER,

FLOORING,
   PORCH MATERIAL, ETC.;
      HARDWARE,
         NAILS,
            EAVES TROUGH,
               DOWN SPOUT,
                  PAINT
                     AND VARNISH

At Your Option: Steam Heating, Furnace Heating, Plumbing Outfit, Electric Wiring, Gas and Electric Fixtures, Wall Paper and Electric Lighting Plants Furnished Extra.

See how much more convenient this is than to be compelled to go to a dozen places for as many different items, each transaction requiring time, expense and worry.

Hardware

Eaves Trough and Down Spouts

THE LANGSTON CUT AND FITTED $1,630.00

Plumbing

Heating

Lighting Fixtures

Building Paper and Roofing

In addition to saving you time and worry in selecting, pricing, etc., you can be sure when you send us your order for a Modern Home that you will make a considerable saving. Thousands of our customers who have built houses according to our plans and with our materials in almost every state of the Union have proved this to their own satisfaction.

You can even go further and benefit yourself still more by including in your order not only all of the materials for your Modern Home as illustrated on this page, but by adding to your order to be shipped when convenient to you, your rugs, furniture, perhaps a piano, a Silvertone phonograph, chinaware, silverware, suits, dresses, linen, etc., all of which you will find illustrated, described and priced in this catalog.

Doesn't it seem reasonable to you that because we very much desire all of your patronage year in and year out, we should be very particular when selling you a Modern Home to give you the best that money can buy for this purpose? A large number of our customers deal with us regularly for their everyday needs because of the splendid material we gave them for their Modern Homes and the substantial savings our prices enabled them to make.

Look over the houses illustrated and priced on the inside back cover of this book—our big General Catalog No. 139. Note the prices for all of the material "Already Cut" and Fitted, then sit down and write us a letter or use the post card opposite page 888 for our beautifully illustrated new Book of "Honor Bilt" Modern Homes, which will be mailed to you postpaid on request.

Paint and Varnishes

Wall Paper

looks more like an authentic pagoda than a practical modern dwelling (Fig. 200), but it depicts a house that was actually built on Long Island, where it ended up looking not quite so Japanese.[8] A bungalow with the same exaggerated parasol roofline and exposed rafters stands among more mundane bungalows at Beachwood on the New Jersey shore (Fig. 201). A careful examination suggests that it is probably the top two stages of the *Bungalow Magazine* design.

The fact that bungalows came in a variety of styles is proven

Fig. 200. Henry Wilson published both The Bungalow Magazine *and two editions of* The Bungalow Book *(1910 and 1923), popularizing the bungalow in its many stylistic guises. (Art and Architecture Collection, Miriam and Ira D. Wallach Division of Art, Prints and Photographs, The New York Public Library, Astor, Lenox, and Tilden Foundations)*

Fig. 201. The pavilionlike second story and the gracefully flared eaves of this bungalow were probably inspired by the January 1910 issue of The Bungalow Magazine.

by one of the most distinctive Sears houses. Because of its Federal Revival portico the Crescent is easily recognizable wherever it was built (Fig. 202). Although Colonial Revival detailing is not usually associated with bungalows, the Crescent was most definitely a bungalow in form, and was so identified in the Sears advertising copy. Its appearance was in keeping with its year of introduction, 1921. By then interest in Period Revival styles (American Colonial and English cottage were dominant) had all but routed the Craftsman mode. The interior of the Crescent emphasized the difference. In place of beamed ceilings, built-in furniture, and chestnut paneling were plain plastered walls trimmed with the simplest moldings.

In 1928 this model could still be purchased for as little as $1,783 "already cut and fitted." At Livingston Manor, where Watson Whittlesey's original houses were Craftsman in appearance, an example of the Crescent was built during a later stage of development (Fig. 203). Even its original trellises, depicted clearly in the catalog illustration, have survived. When the Crescent was built in Riverdale (Fig. 204), its owners chose cobblestone rather than brick piers for the entry, as if indulging a lingering fondness for Craftsman details. Crescents can also be found in Convent Station, Chatham, and Rocky Hill (Fig. 205).

Fig. 202. The Honor-Bilt home named the Crescent was introduced into the Sears catalog of Houses in 1921, and became a best-seller for nearly a decade. (Sears, Roebuck, and Company)

Fig. 203. The Crescent in Highland Park.

Fig. 204. The Crescent in Riverdale.

Fig. 205. The Crescent in Rocky Hill.

During the 1920s the Colonial Revival style accounted for a large percentage of catalog houses built in New Jersey. Sears manufactured a dozen or more variations on the Dutch Colonial theme, identifiable by a gambrel or mock-gambrel roof. Typical was the Oak Park, introduced in 1926 (Fig. 206). Its three-bay facade with side-hall entry is found in neighborhood after neighborhood. The one-story sunroom specified in the catalogue can be seen on an example built in Morris Plains (Fig. 207), a town that sustained intense suburban expansion in the 1920s.

A slightly larger colonial model was the Lexington, built on the venerable center-hall plan (Fig. 208). The catalog language that Sears used to describe this model reflected the shift in values from individualistic Arts and Crafts to conservative Colonial:

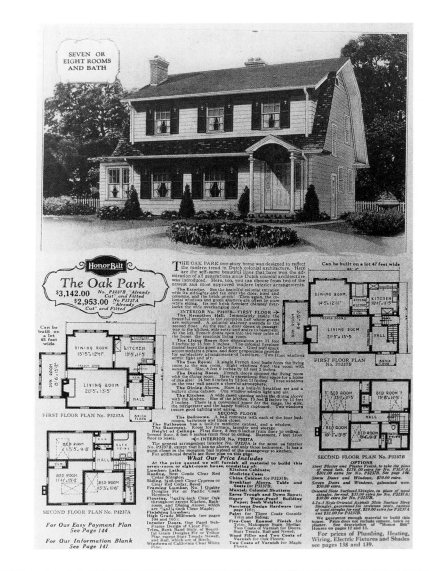

Fig. 206. Like the Crescent, the Oak Park incorporated features of early American architecture, such as the gambrel roof and a pedimented front portico, to appeal to a public increasingly interested in the art and architecture of the nation's past. (Sears, Roebuck, and Company)

Fig. 207. The Oak Park was introduced in the Sears Catalog of Houses in 1926 and was a quick success in a rapidly developing automobile suburb like Morris Plains.

The Lexington is an imposing and dignified study in modern colonial architecture. Observe the wide expanse of pure white, contrasted with green shutters and the red brick chimneys. Observe, also, the stately colonial hooded porch, supported by a pair of slender columns, in perfect harmony with the rest. The side porch, with its many columns and railed roof completes the interesting exterior.

In Rahway, local builder Hank Peare constructed the Lexington from a Sears "kit" for Mr. and Mrs. Ross Nichols in 1929 (Fig. 209). After more than sixty years its dignified appearance is enhanced by mature landscaping, which adds to an impression far removed from the popular notion of a catalog house. Among its many suburban locations, the Lexington was also built in Chatham. There its owners added two flanking wings to create a sizable and unusually customized result.

Despite the popularity of conservative Colonial Revival and English-derived styles, the taste for unusual designs had not vanished entirely with the Japanese-influenced bungalow. In 1929 Sears introduced the San Jose (Fig. 210), one of several Mission-inspired houses "derived from a time when old Spain ruled our southern Pacific coast." Although nothing might seem more unlikely than a southern California house in northern New Jersey, the San Jose was built in the old iron-industry town of Boonton not long after its first catalog appearance (Fig. 211).

Without a doubt catalogs for precut houses were the successors

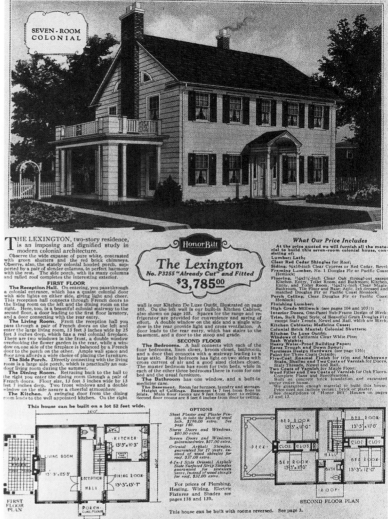

Fig. 208. The Lexington was introduced in 1928. It became one of the most popular of the Sears "center-hall Colonials." (Sears, Roebuck, and Company)

to traditional pattern books. They not only supplied a variety of plans and styles but also provided technical information about construction techniques and even interior decorating ideas. Although Sears, Roebuck was unquestionably the leader in the field, others enjoyed a share of the market as well. In New Jersey a company named Harris Brothers operated a factory in Cresskill, but Sears's only serious competition remained Aladdin. The catalog for 1918–1919 shows that Aladdin's designs were generally simpler and more conservative than those created by Sears. Many were for modest bungalows. Others were for the bungalow's primary low-cost competitor. Nameless in its own day, this kind of house has recently been termed the Foursquare. Its popularity was recognized in a

Fig. 209. The Lexington remains as modestly impressive today as when it was built over sixty years ago.

1914 advertisement for Lowe Brothers Paint, which claimed that "the square house with low roof is probably the most common type of residence in building today. This is due to its economy, both of construction and continued care." Most Foursquares were not really cubical, but were likely to share a handful of nearly obligatory features. A Sears model called the Castleton (Fig. 212) illustrated three: a dormered hipped roof, a full-facade porch, and contrasting siding materials on first and second floors. Like the "rows and rows of bungalows" of a popular song, Foursquare houses were often built in groups in New Jersey towns before and after World War I. Among many other towns, Cliffside Park, Maplewood, and Summit have rows and rows of Foursquares (Fig. 213).

FIVE-ROOM SPANISH BUNGALOW

THE SAN JOSE bungalow architecture is derived from the time when old Spain ruled our Southern Pacific Coast. It is another example of combining the beautiful Spanish mission lines, with the latest idea in a splendid floor plan. Adaptable to any section of the country, it offers every modern comfort possible in a design of this kind. There is a double saving in its sturdy "Honor Bilt" construction, and our factory-to-you system. The rooms are carefully planned, providing ample space. The housework is a pleasurable duty. The exterior is sided with stucco, the roof is shingled, and the eaves are stucco. Among the attractive features are the tower with its grilled windows, the louvre in the gables, batten shutters that serve as a decoration to the French windows, and swinging gate in the arched passageway that leads to the side entry.

The Vestibule. A French door welcomes you into the hospitable San Jose. A coat closet is at the left, another door leads to the kitchen, so that the busy housewife can greet callers without the need of going through the living room, and to the right is a plastered arch opening to the living room.

The Living Room. Floor space, 14 feet 3 inches by 17 feet 5 inches. In the center of the right wall is a mantel and fireplace, with a high sash on either side. Here, the book lover comes into his own, for next to the fireplace are book shelves. Triple French windows provide light and ventilation. Plenty of wall space for a piano, and the usual customary furniture.

The Dining Room is entered from the living room through a plastered arch wide opening. Here, a bay, with a triple window on the right wall, give this room a pleasing air. Floor space, 13 feet 5 inches by 10 feet 4 inches.

The Kitchen. To the left of the dining room is a swinging door that connects with the delightful kitchen. At your right is a built-in cupboard, and close by is space for a work table. At the left is space for a cabinet, and directly opposite is space for a range. A double window is directly above the space for sink. A door leads to the side entry, which has space for refrigerator, stairs to basement, and door to stoop.

The Bedrooms. A central hall, immediately off the dining room, connects with the two bedrooms and bathroom. Each bedroom has two windows, with cross ventilation, and a clothes closet.

The Bathroom is laid out so that all plumbing fixtures can be roughed-in on one wall, thereby saving installation expense. It has a built-in medicine cabinet, and is lighted by a window.

The Basement. Room for heating plant, laundry and storage.

Height of Ceilings. First floor, 8 feet 6 inches from floor to ceiling. Basement, 7 feet from floor to joists.

Honor Bilt

The San Jose
No. P3268 "Already Cut" and Fitted
$2,138.00

What Our Price Includes

At the price quoted we will furnish all material to build this five-room bungalow, consisting of:

Lumber; Lath;
Roofing, Best Grade Clear Red Cedar Shingles;
Framing Lumber, No. 1 Quality Douglas Fir or Pacific Coast Hemlock;
Flooring, 13⁄16x2¼-inch Clear Oak, Living Room, Dining Room and Vestibule; 13⁄16x2¾-inch Clear Maple, Kitchen and Bathroom; 13⁄16x2¾-inch Clear Douglas Fir or Pacific Coast Hemlock, Balance of Rooms;
Finishing Lumber, High Grade Millwork (see pages 104 and 105);
Interior Doors, Two-Cross Panel Design of White Pine With Fir Panels;
Trim, Back Band Style, of Beautiful Grain Yellow Pine;
Windows of California Clear White Pine;
Medicine Case; Mantel; Book Shelves; Kitchen Cabinets;
Shutters;
Eaves Trough and Down Spout;
Heavy Water-Proof Building Paper;
Sash Weights;
Narcissus Design Hardware (see page 116);
Metal Lath;
Paint for Three Coats Outside Trim;
Shellac and Two Coats Varnish, Interior Trim and Doors;
Wood Filler and Two Coats of Varnish for Oak Floors;
Two Coats of Varnish for Maple and Douglas Fir or Pacific Coast Hemlock Floors.

We guarantee enough material to build this house. Price does not include cement, brick, plaster or stucco. See description of "Honor Bilt" Houses on pages 12 and 13.

For prices of Plumbing, Heating, Wiring and Electric Fixtures or Shades see pages 138 and 139.

Can be built on a lot 33 feet wide

FLOOR PLAN

OPTIONS

Sheet Plaster and Plaster Finish to take the place of wood lath, $123.00 extra. See page 140.
Storm Doors and Windows, $65.00 extra.
Screen Doors and Windows, galvanized wire, $35.00 extra.
Oriental Slate Surfaced Shingles, in place of Wood Shingles for roof, $30.00 extra.
4-In-1 Style Oriental Asphalt Slate Surface Strip Shingles, guaranteed for 17 years, instead of Wood Shingles for roof, $23.00 extra.
Oak Trim and Doors for Living Room and Dining Room, $87.00 extra.
For prices of Plumbing, Heating, Wiring and Electric Fixtures or Shades see pages 138 and 139.

For Our Easy Payment Plan See Page 144—For Our Information Blank See Page 141

Fig. 210. Conjuring images of the California missions, the San Jose, introduced by Sears in 1929, was unusually stylish, and, according to its advertising copy, "offers every modern comfort possible." (Sears, Roebuck, and Company)

Also like the bungalow, the Foursquare is not properly a style but a house type. There are Foursquares with Arts and Crafts porches, Mission versions, and Foursquares dressed in Colonial Revival trim. Aladdin's Foursquares, like the Hudson (Fig. 214), tend to be more or less without style, "practical and conservative with no sign of over-trimming," in the words of the copywriter—a neat justification for economical construction. Its very simplicity made the Foursquare easy to embellish. Many builders did so, a practice that increases the difficulty of finding pure catalog examples. One of the many Foursquares in Boonton bears a strong resemblance to Aladdin's Hudson (Fig. 215) with a few differences. Some of the windows have been given diamond-shape panes, and the front porch has been extended around one side. Instead of clapboard,

Fig. 211. It's a long way from southern California to northern New Jersey, but the San Jose made the transition effortlessly.

the walls are shingled, but under its "General Specifications" section, the catalog notes that "shingles for side walls instead of siding will be furnished for any Aladdin dwelling at no extra charge." The ability to sell standardized houses at moderate cost while still allowing buyers to make individualized alterations was surely one of the secrets of Aladdin's and Sears's success.

In method of production, factory-built catalog houses took a step beyond their traditional pattern-book predecessors, but the continuous line of development that links the two is more important than their differences. The connection can be appreciated by examining a single pattern-book environment that developed over a span of fifty years. The Madison neighborhood we looked at in chapter four (see "Building a Pattern-Book Neighborhood") began to be built in the 1880s. Its earliest houses were modest Queen Anne dwellings built from designs published by the Co-operative Building Plan Association. Development continued on into the first two decades of the twentieth century, with owners of the same economic class building simpler houses from designs published by the same company.

By the 1930s, architectural fashion had changed, but the method of architectural choice had not. Instead of turning to architects, the neighborhood continued to rely on books of house patterns. Two houses that still stand at the top of Maple Avenue represent the culmination of the pattern-book phenomenon. One resembles the thousands of Cape Cod houses built after World War II (Fig. 216), while at first glance the other looks like a standard 1950s "center-hall colonial" tract house. Both were barometers of the rise in popularity of the low-cost American colonial house and both were built much earlier than their appearance suggests.

The Cape Cod house was the Attleboro, introduced by Sears, Roebuck in 1933 (Fig. 217). In describing this model Sears boasted of "correct architectural details" (Colonial Williamsburg would open to vistors that same year) and assured prospective builders that there was "no 'gingerbread' to get out of date." Its plan was

Fig. 212. The Castleton from the Sears Catalog of Houses is just one of many variations on the Foursquare house produced by catalogs and individual builders in the 1910s and 1920s. (Sears, Roebuck, and Company)

Fig. 213. The repetition of scale, massing, and setbacks provides a background to the counterpoint of varying window details, porches, and siding materials in a typical suburban neighborhood of Foursquares.

compact and efficient, but conservative when compared to Stickley's free-flowing rooms. One year later Sears introduced the Newcastle, the second of the two Maple Avenue houses, with a claim that "the original Richards House, built at Litchfield, Conn. in 1730 . . . has details almost identical."

These colonial-style houses, the earlier Craftsman homes, the bungalow, the Foursquare, and the small Period Revival house merchandised so successfully by Sears, Roebuck and Aladdin in the 1910s and 1920s were merely different expressions of the continuing pattern-book search for good housing for the largest number of Americans. Because of their mass-production capabilities, the factory-built manufacturers set a new standard for affordable shelter. Constructed in record time of top-quality materials, their houses really did fulfill most of their ambitious advertising claims. For the first time in the history of American building they incorporated all of the features we have come to take for granted as essentials of the

Fig. 214. One of the most basic versions of a Foursquare, the Hudson was produced as a Readi-Cut House by the Aladdin Company in the 1910s.

Fig. 215. This shingle-sided Foursquare is a bit more decorative than most, proving the adapatability of the house to a great range of income levels and stylistic preferences.

Fig. 216. *Now flanked by later additions that respect the character of the original design, the core of this suburban house is clearly the Attleboro from Sears.*

Fig. 217. *The interest in historic American architecture, and the decline in popularity of Craftsman-influenced design is evident in the Attleboro, introduced in 1933 in one of the last Sears Catalogs of Houses ever issued. (Sears, Roebuck, and Company)*

middle-class modern dwelling: efficient planning, a fully integrated system of heating, plumbing, and lighting, and "hygienic" kitchens and bathrooms.

The dream of ever better, ever more reasonably priced housing for every American evaporated with the onset of the Great Depression. New construction ground to a halt as industries closed, unemployment climbed, and many of the nation's banks failed, taking with them the savings of countless potential home buyers. Sears, Aladdin, and other mail-order firms continued producing new designs for a time, but to no avail.

In 1940 Sears finally admitted defeat and abandoned its housing division. Not until after World War II did the housing industry recover. By then a dramatically altered social and economic landscape meant that pattern books and their mail-order offspring were a thing of the past.[9] Two hundred years of building by the book had come to a close.

Arts and Crafts Interiors

The Arts and Crafts interior, especially the Craftsman interior designed and promoted by Gustav Stickley, was based on elimination rather than addition. Stickley's reductionism was not intended for austerity's sake but to provide an appropriate stage for his vision of the rewarding domestic life. His rooms were like the furniture that had first brought him success. Both were meant to reveal rather than conceal structure and materials (Fig. 218). Craftsman furniture in Craftsman rooms was a combination designed to produce a total environment. All this was to be achieved without applied ornament or the excesses of conspicuous consumption.

As a preface to his 1909 book, *Craftsman Homes*, Stickley reprinted an essay by two English architects whose houses and philosophy he admired. In "The Art of Building a Home," Barry Parker and Raymond Unwin admonished their readers to "let us have in our houses rooms where there shall be space to carry on the business of life freely and with pleasure, with furniture made for use; rooms where a drop of water spilled is not fatal; where the life of a child is not made a burden to it by unnecessary restraint; plain, simple, and ungarnished if necessary, but honest."

"Plain, simple, and honest," three watchwords of the Arts and Crafts interior, referred not only to the simplicity of rooms without

Fig. 218. Stickley's furniture, like his houses, was simple, comfortable, sturdy, and without historical stylistic associations.

gratuitous ornament, but to the layout of rooms as well. Typical of Stickley's planning was a principal floor where living and dining rooms were thrown together to encourage communication and shared family life (Fig. 219). Consigned to the dust heap was the formal parlor. If the plan included a small vestibule or reception hall it was a nod in the direction of climate control rather than formality. Kitchens were planned for the pleasure and efficiency of the woman of the house, who had to manage without servants. Open plans and generous windows flooded rooms with light and air, and porches, sleeping porches, and pergolas mimimized barriers between indoors and out. The modernity of Stickley's open plans contrasted starkly with the constricted organization of rooms in many of the mass-produced houses built concurrently (Fig. 220).

As we have seen already, the hearth, and especially the inglenook, was the focal point of most Craftsman homes. In the Vaill house in Oradell (see Fig. 183) is an unusually direct execution of an inglenook design for a small house. Stickley's 1910 view of the living room for House No. 104 was typical of how interiors were presented in *The Craftsman* (Fig. 221). In this design the inglenook occupied one entire short wall of the living room. It became, in effect, a room within the larger room, imparting a sense of cozy enclosure that contrasted with the open plan.

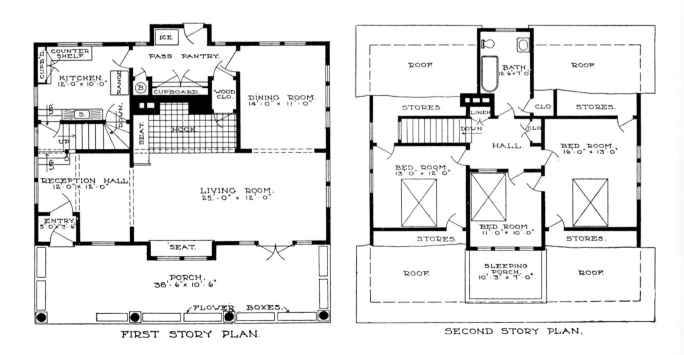

Fig. 219. A typical floor plan from a Craftsman house displays dominant fireplace and hearth, and main rooms separated from each other by only the smallest suggestion of a wall.

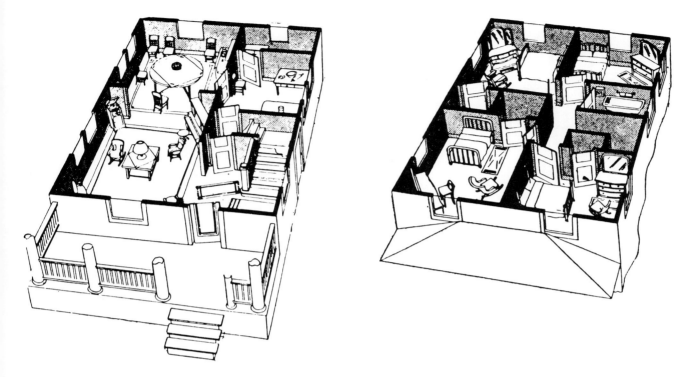

Fig. 220. The floor plan of Aladdin's Readi-Built House, the Hudson.

The separate elements of this particular inglenook were a brick mantel flanked by built-in bookcases below small windows, two built-in cushioned benches, and narrow screen-walls with open shelves to separate the fireplace nook from the larger room. In a brilliant design stroke, Stickley extended the tiled hearth to become the floor of the entire inglenook. The living room as the Vaills built it incorporates every one of these features (Fig. 222).

Stickley's ideal Craftsman interior was one where rooms and furniture expressed the same design attitude. Not everyone who lived in a Craftsman interior subscribed to such a purist outlook, however. In one of Herbert Hapgod's many Arts and Crafts–influenced houses at Mountain Lakes, we can see what the bare bones of a typical room looked like before the house was occupied (see Fig. 188). We also have the rare opportunity to see the same room decorated in period. Its Edwardian combination of furnishings conveys a strong Arts and Crafts flavor despite an array of furniture and objects more eclectic than Stickley might have endorsed (Fig. 223). The truth, of course, is that this view shows more about the reality of most people's taste than the perfect interiors illustrated in *The Craftsman*.

Fig. 221. Interior view of the living room of Craftsman House No. 104, published in December 1910.

Fig. 222. Interior view of the living room of Craftsman House No. 104 as built in New Jersey in 1911. (Ray Stubblebine)

Fig. 223. This early twentieth-century photograph of a Craftsman-style house interior shows American interior design still in transition from the clutter of the Victorian era to the spare decoration anticipated by the design of the house itself. (John Steen, Mountain Lakes Landmarks Committee)

Gustav Stickley

In 1908, northern New Jersey, part rural and part suburban, drew Gustav Stickley from Syracuse, New York. In a part of Morris Plains that is now Parsippany, he created Craftsman Farms, a six-hundred-acre working farm where he hoped to establish a school for boys. The log house he built there was designed as a clubhouse for the farm-school, where visitors, staff, and students could enjoy communal life. Instead it became the Stickley family home when his wife and children took up residence in 1910, and thus became the perfect expression of Stickley's ideas about the ideal domestic environment.

As furniture designer, manufacturer, publisher, and social critic, Gustav Stickley (1857–1942) was the most influential spokesman for the Arts and Crafts movement in America. From 1901 until 1916 his magazine, *The Craftsman*, preached a new American aesthetic. In its pages Stickley promoted his own designs for houses and furnishings meant to create beautiful and harmonious surroundings for the middle class. He published as well the work of leading British and American architects, always setting house and garden in the larger frame of reformist ideals in art, politics, and culture.

In 1903 Stickley became one of the last important creators of pattern-book architecture when he began publishing in every issue of *The Craftsman* two designs for modest dwellings. These he later collected in two book-length volumes, *Craftsman Homes* (1909) and *More Craftsman Homes* (1912). The impact of his house designs is just beginning to be reappraised through an invesigation of built examples. Although it enjoyed national circulation, *The Craftsman* was especially influential in New York and New Jersey. Not only did Stickley live in New Jersey, but his magazine was published in Manhattan, where readers could visit the thirteen-story Craftsman building, the Con-

ran's of its day. There, in addition to his editorial and architectural offices, Stickley had furniture and design showrooms, product and garden displays, a clubroom, library, and lecture hall, as well as a top-floor restaurant.

By 1917 changes in American taste and his own overextended design empire forced Stickley into bankruptcy. He lost everything, including his beloved Craftsman Farms, down to the last chair and hand-embroidered table runner, but not before his designs for Craftsman homes had made a lasting mark on New Jersey's suburbs.

Notes

CHAPTER ONE

From Builders' Books to Pattern Books

1. Stephen Youngs, Memorandum Book, 1793–1867, The Joint Free Public Library of Morristown and Morris Township, Morristown, N.J.
2. Martha Daingerfield Bland to Frances Bland Randolph, 12 May 1777, quoted by Cam Cavanaugh, *In Lights and Shadows: Morristown in Three Centuries* (Morristown, N.J.: The Joint Free Public Library of Morristown and Morris Township, 1986), 40.
3. Thomas Thompson, *A Letter from New Jersey, in America, Giving Some Account and Description of that Province* (London, 1756), cited by Oral S. Coad, *New Jersey in Travelers Accounts* (Metuchen, N.J.: The Scarecrow Press, 1972), 16.
4. Millicent Sowerby, *Catalogue of the Library of Thomas Jefferson* (Washington, D.C.: University Press of Virginia, 1952–1959).
5. Willard Sterne Randall, *The Proprietary House in Amboy* (Perth Amboy, N.J.: Proprietary House Association, 1975), 20 and 24.
6. J. E. Pryor, Account Book, New-York Historical Society.
7. Barry John Brady, National Register of Historic Places Nomination for Fenwick Manor (Trenton, N.J.: Office of New Jersey Heritage, 1990).
8. Alexis de Tocqueville, *Democracy in America* (Garden City, N.Y.: Doubleday, 1969), 78.
9. Martha Hopler, Edward Roessler, and Wallace West, *The Mendhams* (Brookside, N.J.: The Mendham Township Committee, 1964), 93.
10. William H. Benedict, *New Brunswick in History* (New Brunswick, N.J.: W. H. Benedict, 1925), 150.

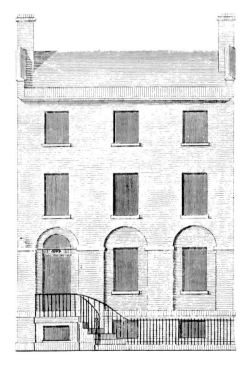

11. Ibid.
12. *Dictionary of American Biography* (New York: Charles Scribner's Sons, 1964), 481.
13. Constance M. Greiff, Mary W. Gibbons, and Elizabeth G. C. Menzies, *Princeton Architecture* (Princeton, N.J.: Princeton University Press, 1967), 92.
14. Theodore Dwight, *Things as They Are* (New York, 1834), quoted in Warren S. Tryon, ed., *A Mirror for Americans: Life and Manners in the United States, 1790–1870, as Recorded by American Travelers* (Chicago: University of Chicago Press: 1952), 1:125.
15. *The Builder* 10 (London, 15 May 1852): 315.
16. Randall, *Proprietary House*, 16–19.
17. *Alexander Papers*, Collection of the New-York Historical Society, 1763, Box 11.
18. Stephen Youngs, Memorandum Book.

CHAPTER TWO

The Pattern Book Comes of Age

1. Stephen Youngs, Memorandum Book, 1793–1867, The Joint Free Public Library of Morristown and Morris Township, Morristown, N.J.
2. Cam Cavanaugh, Barbara Hoskins, and Frances D. Pingeon, *At Speedwell in the Nineteenth Century* (Morristown, N.J.: The Speedwell Village, 1981), 35.
3. Ibid., 82.
4. Stephanie Potash, "Judge Francis Lathrop," typewritten ms. (Madison, N.J., 1990), 6.
5. Heritage Studies, Inc., "Acorn Hall Preservation Plan: Part I" (Morristown, N.J.: Morris County Historical Society, 1980), 5–6.
6. Jane B. Davies, "Downing and Davis: Collaborators in the Picturesque," in George B. Tatum and Elisabeth Blair MacDougal, eds., *Prophet with Honor, The Career of Andrew Jackson Downing*, Dumbarton Oaks Colloquium on the History of Landscape Architecture II (Philadelphia: The Athenaeum of Philadelphia, 1989), 88.
7. Downing thought enough of Wheeler to publish two of his designs in *The Architecture of Country Houses* (1850) and to quote him at length. The following year, however, when he reviewed *Rural Homes* in *The Horticulturist*, he roundly criticized Wheeler's claim to have designed specifically American houses.
8. George B. Thomas and Carol Doebly, *Cape May, Queen of the Seaside Resorts* (Cranbury, N.J.: Associated University Presses, 1976), ii.
9. F. L. Mott, *A History of American Magazines, 1741–1850* (Cambridge, Mass.: Harvard University Press, 1930), quoted by Charles B. Wood III, "The New 'Pattern Books' and the Role of the Agricultural Press," in Tatum and MacDougal, *Prophet with Honor*, 165.
10. Ursula Brecknell, National Register of Historic Places Nomination

for River Road Historic District (Trenton, N.J.: Office of New Jersey Heritage, 1990).

11. A. J. Downing, *Cottage Residences* (New York: Dover Publications reprint of 1873 edition, 1981), 24.

12. Constance M. Greiff points out in Short and Ford, Architects, "The Hermitage, Historic Structure Report" (Ho-Ho-Kus, N.J.: Friends of the Hermitage, Inc., 1981), 34, that "in many respects Ranlett was in the forefront of the transformation of taste that took place in the early Victorian era. None of the publications that appeared earlier than his exhibit such a freely asymmetrical version of the Gothic Revival as the Hermitage." Greiff's point is confirmed by Design XIX in the 1850 edition of *The Architecture of Country Houses*. Its plan and principal elevation are so similar to those of the Hermitage that it is difficult to imagine that A. J. Davis, who improved Downing's original sketch for this engraving, was ignorant of Ranlett's design.

13. Lewis F. Allen, *Rural Architecture* (New York: Lewis F. Allen, 1852), from the introduction, unpaginated.

CHAPTER THREE

New Technologies, New Styles

1. Walker Field, "A Reexamination into the Invention of the Balloon Frame," *Journal of the Society of Architectural Historians* 1 (October 1942): 3–29.

2. Solon Robinson, quoted in George E. Woodward, *Woodward's Country Homes* (New York: Geo. E. Woodward, 1865), 151.

3. Woodward, *Country Homes*, 154–155.

4. Field, in "A Reexamination," makes all these points about the balloon frame, 36.

5. *New York Tribune*, 3 November 1873, quoted by Lawrence Korinda, "Profile of Boonton" (Independent Senior Study, Carnegie-Mellon University, 1975), 16.

6. William Bailey Lang, *Views with Ground Plans of the Highland Cottages at Roxbury* (Boston: Bugham and Felch, 1845), unpaginated.

7. Mark Ehrlich, *With Our Own Hands* (Philadelphia: Temple University Press, 1987), 55.

8. *Snell's History of Hunterdon and Somerset Counties* (Philadelphia: Evert and Peck, 1881), 251.

9. Terry Karschner, National Register of Historic Places Nomination for Fordville (Trenton, N.J.: Office of New Jersey Heritage, 1977).

10. Constance M. Greiff in Short and Ford, Architects, "The Hermitage, Historic Structure Report" (Ho-Ho-Kus, N.J.: Friends of the Hermitage, Inc., 1981), 35.

11. Quoted by Charles Lockwood in *Bricks and Brownstone* (New York: McGraw-Hill, 1972), 163.

12. Cumberland County Register of Historic Sites and Structures, 1980, No. C22.

CHAPTER FOUR

Eclecticism Prevails

1. *Scientific American Architects and Builders Edition*, June 1886, 41.
2. Gustav Kobbe, *The Central Railroad of New Jersey* (Gustav Kobbe: New York, 1890).
3. *New York Herald*, 19 April 1877, quoted by Henry Hudson Holly, *Modern Dwellings in Town and Country* (New York: Harper and Brothers, 1878), 21.
4. Henry-Russell Hitchcock, *American Architectural Books: A List of Books, Portfolios, and Pamphlets on Architecture and Related Subjects Published in America Before 1895* (New York: Da Capo Press, 1976).
5. A full account of the building of these houses is furnished by Melinda McGough in her unpublished typescript, "Three Houses by Samuel Sloan" (no date).
6. *Haddonfield Basket*, 21 December 1874, 27.
7. This house was identified as Anderson's in the Wallingford section of the Bergen County Historic Sites Survey, 1982, maintained by the Bergen County Office of Cultural and Historic Affairs.
8. Holly, *Modern Dwellings in Town and Country*, 20.
9. See Michael A. Tomlan's introduction to *Palliser's Late Victorian Architecture* (Watkins Glen, N.Y.: American Life Foundation, 1978).
10. This contract is in the collection of the Middletown Township (N.J.) Historical Society.
11. Robert W. Shoppell, ed., *Shoppell's Modern Houses* 1 (January 1886): 2.
12. Ibid., 1.
13. Ibid., 1.
14. Shoppell, *Shoppell's Modern Houses* 50 (1896): advertising supplement.
15. Shoppell, *Shoppell's Modern Houses* 41 (1894): vii.
16. W. W. Munsell and Company, *Biographical and Genealogical History of Morris County* (New York: W. W. Munsell and Co., 1882), 544.
17. The description comes from the text accompanying Design No. 346 in *Shoppell's Modern Houses* 1 (July 1886).
18. Anna Blair Titman Cummins, *Cummins-Titman and Allied Families* (Hartford, Conn.: States Historical Company, Inc., 1946).
19. For a discussion of George F. Barber's career see Michael A. Tomlan's introduction to the reissue of *Barber's Cottage Souvenir No. 2* (Watkins Glen, N.Y.: American Life Foundation, 1982).
20. Barber, *Cottage Souvenir No. 2*, 9.
21. William A. Lambert, *Suburban Architecture* (New York City: privately printed, 1894), introduction.
22. Gervase Wheeler's cruciform plan included a traditional stair hall to the left of the parlor. When he adapted Wheeler's design, Joseph Warren Revere dispensed with the partition between stair hall and parlor so that the parlor contained the stair. This condition may be the earliest American example of what grew into the full-blown Queen Anne living hall.

FRONT ELEVATION

CHAPTER FIVE

Back to Basics

1. "A Visit to Craftsman Farms," *The Craftsman*, September 1910, 638.
2. Ibid., 640.
3. "Craftsman Houses for Home Builders," *The Craftsman*, April 1913, 89.
4. Diefenthaler family correspondence, courtesy Betty Diefenthaler, Chatham, N.J.
5. "Craftsman Houses for Small Families," *The Craftsman*, December 1910, 294.
6. Ray Stubblebine, National Register of Historic Places Nomination for Edward Vaill House (Trenton, N.J.: Office of New Jersey Heritage, 1990).
7. For a comprehensive discussion of the bungalow and its design evolution see Clay Lancaster, *The American Bungalow* (New York: Abbeville Press, 1985).
8. Lancaster, in *The American Bungalow*, discovered the connection between the *Bungalow Magazine* cover design and the Long Island example, 91–94.
9. Pattern-book–like plans are found in newspapers and magazines today, of course. Our thanks to Constance Greiff for bringing up this point.

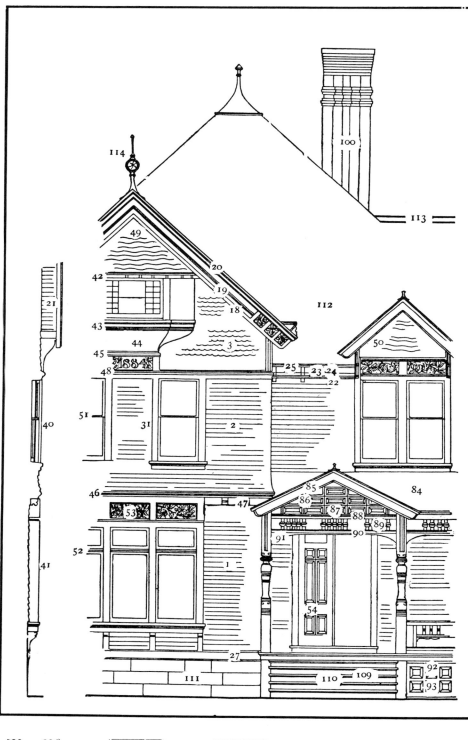

BODY
1. *First story*
2. *Second story*
3. *Attic*

CORNICE
18.–20. Bargeboard
18. *Face rafter margin*
19. *Face rafter mold*
20. *Eaves mold*
21. *Ceiling under eaves*
23. *Gutter face*
24. *Gutter brackets*
25. *Gutter cap*

27. WATER TABLE

WINDOW FRAME
40. *Reveal*
41. *Edge*

ATTIC WINDOW
42. *Cornice*
43. *Sill mold*
44. *Cove*
45. *Base mold*

46. BELT COURSE

47. BEAM ENDS

48. MOLD UNDER ATTIC

49. GABLE OVER ATTIC WINDOW

50. DORMER GABLE

51. WINDOW SASH

52. WINDOW TRANSOM

DOOR
54. *Stiles and rails*

PORCH
84. *Roof*
85. *Face rafter*
86. *Gable rail*
87. *Gable panels*
88. *Plate*
89. *Cornice balusters*
90. *Cornice rail*
91. *Cornice curve or bracket*
92. *Rails below*
93. *Panels below*

CHIMNEY
100. *Shaft*

STEPS
109. *Tread mold*
110. *Riser*

111. FOUNDATION

ROOF
113. *Ridge roll*
114. *Iron finials*

Architectural Glossary

244

CORNICE

4. *Edge of crown mold*
5. *Crown*
6. *Fasciae*
7. *Bed mold*
8. *Dentals*
9. *Frieze*
10. *Panel mold*
11. *Panel*
12. *Architrave*
13. *Sunk face of bracket*
14. *Raised face of bracket*
15. *Bracket panel*
16. *Bracket margin*
17. *Soffit*

26. CORNER BOARD

WATER TABLE

28. *Slope*
29. *Edge*
30. *Face*

WINDOW

32. *Face*	38. *Sill*
33. *Cap fillet*	39. *Apron*
34. *Cap mold*	40. *Reveal*
35. *Cap panel*	41. *Edge*
36. *Keystone*	51. *Sash*
37. *Chamfer*	52. *Transom*

DOOR

54. *Stiles and rails*
55. *Mold*
56. *Projecting part of panel*
57. *Receding part of panel*

BLINDS

58. *Slats*
59. *Frame*

PORCH

60. *Balustrade post*
61. *Balustrade base*
62. *Balustrade rail*
63. *Receding part of baluster*
64. *Projecting part of baluster*
65. *Abacus*
66. *Capital*
67. *Neck mold*
68. *Chamfer*
69. *Shaft*
70. *Rosette*
71. *Plinth*
72. *Plinth mold*
73. *Rail*
74. *Dado*
75. *Dado panel*
76. *Base*
77. *Base mold*
78. *Ornamental rail*
79. *Ornamental panel*
80. *Ornamental chamfer*
81. *Bead below steps*
82. *Panel mold below steps*
83. *Panel below steps*

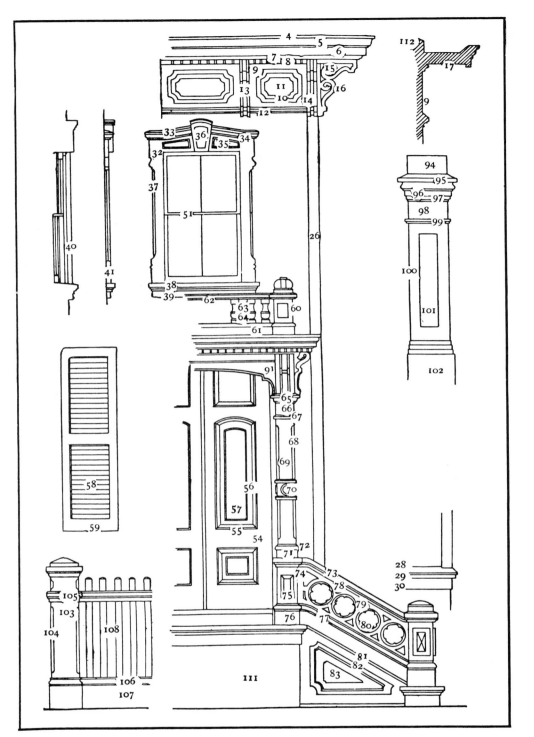

CHIMNEY

94. *Top of cap*
95. *Crown mold of cap*
96. *Faciae of cap*
97. *Bed mold of cap*
98. *Frieze of cap*
99. *Architrave*
100. *Shaft*
101. *Panels*
102. *Base*

FENCE

103. *Post*
104. *Post chamfer*
105. *Upper rail*
106. *Lower rail*
107. *Base*
108. *Pickets*

111. FOUNDATION

112. ROOF

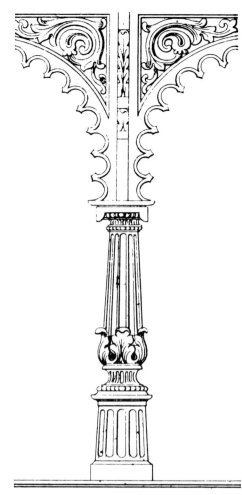

Detail of a porch from Plate XXI, Samuel Sloan's The Model Architect, *1852.*

Detail of a porch in Morristown.

Bibliography

The most definitive list of pattern books, builders' books, and other publications of their kind is found in *American Architectural Books* by the late architectural historian Henry-Russell Hitchcock (Da Capo Press, New York, 1976). It is available in the reference holdings of most large libraries. Hitchcock notes the locations of original copies of the books he lists. Additionally, all of the more than six hundred titles are available on microfilm. Readers should be aware that additional titles have come to light since *American Architectural Books* was published, and the libraries listed have expanded their collections.

In New Jersey, Rutgers University, Princeton University, and the New Jersey Historical Society are repositories for some of the pattern books in the Hitchcock bibliography. In addition, the Newark Public Library has a large collection of original pattern books in its Fine Arts Division.

Three important repositories of original pattern books lie just beyond New Jersey's borders. The New York Public Library has an extensive and surprisingly accessible collection of architectural books. Avery Architectural and Fine Arts Library at Columbia University in the City of New York is one of the greatest architectural libraries in the world. As the result of a farsighted collecting policy, it owns original and microfilm copies of nearly every American architectural book. It has also been a pioneer in the acquisition of building trades catalogues, which further document the designs, hardware, plumbing fixtures, roofing materials, and so forth of American building in the nineteenth and twentieth centuries. Avery Library is open to serious researchers only. A pass for short-

term access must be applied for in writing to Columbia University.

The Athenaeum, a private library established in Philadelphia in 1814, maintains in its 1847 building by John Notman a rich collection of books and related items from the nineteenth century. The collection covers the fine arts, architecture, and decorative arts. Researchers must make appointments.

The beginning researcher interested in American pattern books, or the old-house owner curious about a possible pattern-book source for her own house, may also turn to reprints. Many are low-cost paperbacks; other, more expensive, collectors' editions may be available through libraries. The republication of these books has made important primary source documents of social and architectural history widely available.

In the following bibliography, we have listed only those pattern books that have been reprinted. They are grouped to correspond with the material treated in each chapter of the text, and then arranged chronologically. The reader must remember that a reprint may not be based on the first edition of the title. Where two or more books by one author are collected in a single reprint edition, the date of the latest original work is the date under which the entire reprint is cited.

Builder's Books and Early American Pattern Books

SWAN, ABRAHAM. *The British Architect*. London, 1758. Reprint. New York: Da Capo Press, 1967.

BENJAMIN, ASHER. *The American Builder's Companion*. Sixth edition, 1827. Reprint. New York: Dover Publications, 1969.

BENJAMIN, ASHER. *The Architect, or Practical House Carpenter*. 1830. Reprint. New York: Dover Publications, 1988.

LAFEVER, MINARD. *The Beauties of Modern Architecture*. 1835. Reprint. New York: Da Capo Press, 1968.

LAFEVER, MINARD. *The Modern Builder's Guide*. Third edition, 1846. Reprint. New York: Dover Publications, 1969.

The Golden Age of Pattern Books

DAVIS, ALEXANDER JACKSON. *Rural Residences*. 1837. Reprint. New York: Da Capo Press, 1980.

DOWNING, ANDREW JACKSON. *The Architecture of Country Houses*. 1850. Reprint. New York: Da Capo Press, 1968. Reprint. New York: Dover Publications, 1969.

RANLETT, WILLIAM H. *The Architect*. 2 vols. 1849 (vol. 1) and 1851 (vol. 2). Reprint. New York: Da Capo Press, 1976.

SLOAN, SAMUEL. *The Model Architect*. 1852. Reprint, two volumes. New York: Da Capo Press, 1975.

SLOAN, SAMUEL. *The Model Architect*. 1852. Reprinted, two volumes in one, as *Sloan's Victorian Buildings*. New York: Dover Publications, 1980.

DOWNING, ANDREW JACKSON. *Rural Essays*. Second edition, 1854. Reprint. New York: Da Capo Press, 1975.

SMITH, OLIVER P. *The Domestic Architect*. 1854. Reprinted as *Victorian Domestic Architect*. Watkins Glen, N.Y.: The American Life Foundation, 1978.

VAUX, CALVERT. *Villas and Cottages*. 1857. Reprint. New York: Da Capo Press, 1968.

VAUX, CALVERT. *Villas and Cottages*. 1864 edition. Reprint. New York: Dover Publications, 1970.

SLOAN, SAMUEL. *City and Suburban Architect*. 1859. Reprint. New York: Da Capo Press, 1975.

DOWNING, ANDREW JACKSON. *Cottage Residences*. Fifth edition, 1873. Reprint. New York: Dover Publications, 1981.

Mid-Nineteenth-Century Innovators

FOWLER, ORSON S. *A Home for All*. Revised edition, 1853. Reprint. New York: Dover Publications, 1973.

WOODWARD, GEORGE EVERSTON. *Woodward's Country Homes*. 1865. Reprint. Watkins Glen, N.Y.: The American Life Foundation, 1978.

WOODWARD, GEORGE EVERSTON. *Woodward's National Architect*. 1869. Reprinted as *A Victorian Housebuilder's Guide*. New York: Dover Publications, 1988. Reprinted under its original title by Da Capo Press, 1975, and by The American Life Foundation, 1977.

BICKNELL, A. J. *Bicknell's Village Builder and Supplement*. 1872. Reprint. Watkins Glen, N.Y.: The American Life Foundation, 1976.

CUMMINGS, M. F., AND MILLER, C. C. *Architecture*. 1865. *Architectural Details*. 1873. Reprinted, two books in one, as *Victorian Architectural Details*. Watkins Glen, N.Y.: American Life Foundation, 1980.

BICKNELL, A.J. *Wooden and Brick Buildings with Details*. 1875. Reprint. New York: Da Capo Press, 1977.

Queen Anne and High Victorian Styles

HUSSEY, E. C. *Home Building*. 1875. Reprinted as *Victorian Home Building*. Watkins Glen, N.Y.: The American Life Foundation, 1976.

BICKNELL, A. J. *Bicknell's Village Builder and Supplement*. 1878. Reprinted as *Bicknell's Victorian Buildings*. New York: Dover Publications, 1979.

HOLLY, HENRY HUDSON. *Country Seats*. 1863. *Modern Dwellings*. 1878.

Reprinted, two books in one. Watkins Glen, N.Y.: The American Life Foundation, second ed., 1980.

COMSTOCK, WILLIAM T. *Modern Architectural Designs and Details*. 1881. Reprinted as *Victorian Domestic Architectural Plans and Details*. New York: Dover Publications, 1987.

TUTHILL, WILLIAM B. *Interiors and Interior Details*. 1882. Reprint. Watkins Glen, N.Y.: The American Life Foundation, 1984.

TUTHILL, WILLIAM B. *Interiors and Interior Details*. 1882. Reprint. New York: Da Capo Press, 1975.

COMSTOCK, WILLIAM T. *American Cottages*. 1883. Reprinted as *County Houses and Seaside Cottages of the Victorian Era*. New York: Dover Publications, 1985.

PALLISER, GEORGE, AND PALLISER, CHARLES. *Palliser's New Cottage Homes and Details*. 1887. Reprint. New York: Da Capo Press, 1975.

SHOPPELL, R. W. *Shoppell's Modern Houses*. 1887. Reprint. Rockville Centre, N.Y.: Antiquity Reprints, 1987.

PALLISER, GEORGE, AND PALLISER, CHARLES. *Palliser's New Cottage Homes and Details*. 1887. *American Architecture; or Every Man a Complete Builder*. 1888. Reprinted, two books in one, as *Palliser's Late Victorian Architecture*. Watkins Glen, N.Y.: The American Life Foundation, 1978.

SHELDON, GEORGE WILLIAM, ED. *Artistic Country Seats*. 1886–1887. Reprint, two volumes. New York: Da Capo Press, 1979.

BARBER, GEORGE F. *The Cottage Souvenier No. 2*. 1891. Reprint. Watkins Glen, N.Y.: The American Life Foundation, 1982.

COMSTOCK, WILLIAM T. *Suburban and Country Homes*. 1893. Reprint. Rockville Centre, N.Y.: Antiquity Reprints, 1984.

HOPKINS, D. S. *Houses and Cottages*. 1893. Reprint. Rockville Centre, N.Y.: Antiquity Reprints, 1983.

CARPENTRY AND BUILDING MAGAZINE. *Modern American Dwellings*. 1897. Reprint. Rockville Centre, N.Y.: Antiquity Reprints, 1984.

SHOPPELL, ROBERT W. *Building Designs*. 1890 (Selected).
Shoppell's Modern Houses. Jan.-Mar. 1890.
Shoppell's Modern Houses. No. 68, 1900.
Reprinted, three volumes in one, as *Turn-of-the-Century Houses, Cottages and Villas*. New York: Dover Publications, 1983.

Craftsman Homes and Catalog Houses

STICKLEY, GUSTAV. *Craftsman Homes*. 1909. Reprint. New York: Dover Publications, 1979.

STICKLEY, GUSTAV. *More Craftsman Homes*. 1912. Reprint. New York: Dover Publications, 1982.

COMSTOCK, WILLIAM PHILLIPS, AND SCHERMERHORN, CLARENCE EATON. *Bungalows, Camps and Mountain Houses*. 1915. Reprint. Washington, D.C.: The American Institute of Architects Press, 1990.

ALADDIN COMPANY. *Aladdin Homes Built in a Day, Catalog No. 31*. 1919. Reprint. Watkins Glen, N.Y.: The American Life Foundation, 1985.

SEARS, ROEBUCK AND CO. *Sears, Roebuck Catalog of Houses*. 1926. Reprint. New York: Dover Publications, 1991.

JONES, ROBERT T. *Small Houses of Architectural Distinction*. 1929. Reprint. New York: Dover Publications, 1987.

In addition to the reproduced pattern books themselves are several books that contain portions of pattern books or illustrations from pattern books accompanied by modern text.

BERG, DONALD, ED. *Country Patterns*. Pittstown, N.J.: Main Street Press, 1986. (Nineteenth-century plans and patterns for rural dwellings, outbuildings, and directions for crafts and decoration.)

GROW, LAWRENCE. *Old House Plans: Two Centuries of American Domestic Architecture*. New York: Universe Books, 1987. (Contains sample illustrations from some of the less-well-known building design sources, including *The American Agriculturalist* and *Peale's Popular Educator*.)

GROW, LAWRENCE. *More Classic Old House Plans: Authentic Designs for Colonial and Victorian Homes*. Pittstown, N.J.: Main Street Press, 1986. (Just as the title suggests, more plans and elevations taken from American architectural books of the period.)

LEWIS, ARNOLD. *American Country Houses of the Gilded Age*. New York: Dover Publications, 1982. (Reprint of illustrations from G. W. Sheldon, *Artistic County Seats*, 1887, with new text.)

MITCHELL, EUGENE, ED. *American Victoriana*. San Francisco: Chronicle Books, 1979. (Selections from *Scientific American Architect and Builders Edition*, 1880–1905.)

MOSS, ROGER. *Century of Color, 1820–1920*. Watkins Glen, N.Y.: The American Life Foundation, 1981. (Rare color plates from several pattern books and other sources illustrate American architecture and the colors it was intended to be painted.)

STEVENSON, KATHERINE COLE, AND JANDL, H. WARD. *Houses By Mail: A Guide to Houses from Sears, Roebuck, and Company*. Washington, D.C.: The Preservation Press, 1986. (A compilation of the *Sears Catalog of Houses* from 1908 through 1939.)

STICKLEY, GUSTAV, ED. *Craftsman Bungalows: 59 Homes from "The Craftsman."* New York: Dover Publications, 1988. (Houses, interior decoration, and landscape advice from Stickley's magazine of 1903–1916 that did not appear in his two books of house plans, *Craftsman Homes* and *More Craftsman Homes*.)

Index

(Italic numbers indicate illustrations.)